Ten-Mile Morning

My Journey through Anorexia Nervosa

Adam Lamparello

Hamilton Books

A member of
The Rowman & Littlefield Publishing Group
Lanham • Boulder • New York • Toronto • Plymouth, UK

Published by Hamilton Books
4501 Forbes Boulevard, Suite 200, Lanham, Maryland 20706

10 Thornbury Road, Plymouth PL6 7PP, United Kingdom

Hamilton Books Acquisitions Department (301) 459-3366

British Library Cataloging in Publication Information Available

Library of Congress Control Number: 2011942535
ISBN 978-0-7618-5803-4 (pbk : alk. paper) -- ISBN 978-0-7618-5804-1 (electronic)

The paper used in this publication meets the minimum requirements of American National Standard for Information Sciences Permanence of Paper for Printed Library Materials, ANSI Z39.48-1992.

Printed in the United States of America

This book is dedicated to Elvis Presley

"The image is one thing and the human being is another . . . it's very hard to live up to an image."

Thanks Mom and Dad . . . for everything.
I love you

This is a true story. The names of people and locations of places have been changed to protect the identity of those who were a part of my life during this difficult time.

Contents

Preface

This book details my five-year struggle with anorexia nervosa, from 2006 through the present, and how I am recovering from the illness and gaining self-acceptance, self-love, and nurturing healthy relationships with food, people, and myself. The book is extraordinarily graphic in describing the events that led up to my struggle with anorexia. It is all part of the story that resulted in my need to exercise control over my body and weight through starvation. To those of you who are struggling with eating disorders, I know your pain; I experienced it myself, but I also know liberation, freedom, and the ability to obtain true happiness on my own terms. I hope this book helps you to get to that place or at least get on the journey to that place. My goal in writing this book is to help all those afflicted with eating disorders realize that you can get better and live the happy and fulfilling life that you've always dreamed of.

Introduction

I never knew Elvis Presley personally, though I wish I had. I love his music, but that is not why I decided to dedicate this book to him. I don't believe that Elvis died simply from taking too many drugs. I think the drug consumption was a symptom of deeper emotional issues from which he suffered. I think that, similar to people suffering from anorexia, Elvis felt a sense of inadequacy, loneliness, and low self-esteem. But I don't believe that he had the necessary support around him to allow him to confront these issues. I do believe that his inner circle cared about him, but in the end, I think Elvis felt isolated and alone, and that neither his inner circle nor anyone else could help him with the tremendous pain that he suffered inside. The emotional pain that he suffered was, in my opinion, what prompted him to use drugs as a way to "numb out," or suppress those feelings, and over time, those substances caused his death.

Maybe things could have been different. Aside from the fact that there was somewhat of a stigma surrounding psychotherapy back then, I don't think many people understood Elvis as a person. They understood him as an image, as an entertainer, and as an icon. But they didn't realize that he was a human being, with the same faults, flaws, and issues that we all have. His emotional issues were serious and, as with most people affected by eating disorders, very difficult to confront. So, in dedicating this book to Elvis, I hope that I can help some of you who are struggling with anorexia or bulimia, because there is a wonderful life that awaits you after you recover from this disorder.

Chapter One

The Early Years

A Bridge over Troubled Water

I've had failed relationships with two married women. I've been fired from three jobs. I've abused alcohol. I've been addicted to both legal and illegal drugs. I was in a near fatal car accident. I suffered from, and continued to suffer from, depression and insomnia. I've had my heart broken. Sometimes I have thoughts of suicide. The most difficult challenge I ever faced, however, was anorexia nervosa. I didn't just become an anorexic. I had a life filled with disappointment, disillusionment, and disloyalty, as well as severe emotional and psychological traumas. I had no self-esteem, and no ability to accept and love my authentic self. Instead, I was filled with self-hate, insecurity, and feelings of inadequacy. I was the typical "people pleaser," even though my interactions with the people around me made me dislike them even more than I did myself.

Ultimately, I discovered that exercise, weight loss, and starvation gave me the control over my life that I so desperately needed. Anorexia made me feel empowered, strong, and, for the first time, secure. Yet, I was living under a delusion. I was never in control. Anorexia was controlling me, and killing me. My journey with anorexia was a painful process that eventually led to a nervous breakdown. I locked myself in my apartment for eight months, isolated and alone. My weight plummeted to 123 pounds and my body fat percentage to five percent. I screamed and cried for help. I found help from my parents, friends, and treatment team. I am now in recovery, where I am starting to feel liberation, self-acceptance, and self-love. I am telling you my story in the hope that it can help you as you struggle with the difficult days in your life.

As I look back to my early years, I now know that the blueprint for anorexia was sown during my childhood. I remember my life as far back as when I was five years old. I had wonderful, loving, generous, and supportive parents. They always did their best to make me a happy child and to instill in me the types of values that would allow me to be successful on whatever path I chose in adulthood. They taught me the value of hard work, honesty, integrity, and humility. They sacrificed so much of themselves to make their children's lives better. I love them and always will.

Like everyone else, though, my parents were human and they made mistakes. While they always acted with the best intentions, my parents were strict, rather authoritarian, and controlling. Based on their own upbringing and experiences, they viewed the world in a certain way and developed their own set of values, beliefs, and principles. They tried to impart this perspective on me and my siblings.

The problem came in the "control" aspect of the relationship. Even in my early years, I didn't necessarily agree with my parents' worldviews, whether it pertained to God, organized religion, morals, individuality, politics, or other topics. On small matters, I sometimes thought my parents were wrong when they made me go to church and attend Catholic schools, when they punished me too severely, or didn't give much credence to my opinions or attempts at developing my own perspective on the world, people, morality, and other existential issues. I was so young and had so many questions. My parents had the answers, and I think they expected that we would always accept those answers as true. I don't think they liked it when we disagreed or challenged them. They liked to control the family dynamic, and in many ways, that set the stage for my being reluctant to assert myself, and to use my voice to draw boundaries with other people.

Sadly, I was an overly sensitive child. Even the slightest criticism would cut through me like a knife. If my mom was dissatisfied with a grade I received in school or at how I behaved around other people, I would feel horrible. If my dad was angry at me for any reason, I felt awful. I wanted to please them in any way that I could. I would do anything. I loved them. I tried at all costs to avoid the shame, guilt, and embarrassment that accompanied a criticism or punishment. I just wanted to conform to my parents' values and be a good son. I didn't feel like I could speak up, disagree, or get mad at them because I knew that would upset the "control" dynamic. I wanted to be what they wanted me to be. I wanted to have their approval because then I would have self-approval and self-esteem. My happiness was contingent on the approval of my parents — and everyone else.

The problem is that I never developed a sense of self. I never discovered who I was, or what it meant to be "Adam." I was always so busy trying to make others happy that I never discovered what made me happy. I felt under the control of everyone around me, whether it be my family, friends, teachers, or coaches. As a result, I was never in control of my life. I never had the ability to speak up for myself, draw boundaries, or voice my opinion on things that mattered to me. I just did whatever people told me to do, even when I didn't want to. The behavior that I learned in childhood continued into adulthood, as I became the quintessential "people pleaser." I did everything I could to make my co-workers, lovers, and friends like me. My happiness was contingent on everything external, whether it was the happiness of others or the achievement of awards and honors.

Not only did I fail to build a relationship with myself, I never had any sense of self-respect, self-acceptance, or self-esteem. I had no inner peace. Instead, I had tremendous self-hatred because I let everyone control and exploit me. I felt this way as early as nine years into my life. I became a "fake" person who put on an image that I knew everyone would find acceptable and likeable, because I thought that nobody would like the depressed, insecure, self-hating Adam. I led a manufactured existence, and I was wonderful at manipulating relationships to avoid the shame that I felt when I upset my family. I never wanted to feel those feelings again, and in my adult life, I betrayed everything that was real about me to avoid them. In so doing, I created a life of pure hell. I was miserable. If people only knew the pain I was experiencing. I needed something to make me feel empowered. I needed a friend. Someone that understood me. Someone to give me the confidence that I so yearned for, to fill that empty void inside of me.

I tried to fill that void with married women. I sought to escape my disillusionment with life, people, lawyers, and organized religion by abusing Valium, Vicoden, and Cocaine. I tried to find pleasure at strip clubs and with prostitutes. It was only temporary. My life kept spiraling downward until I suffered a nervous breakdown. Then I discovered something that gave me a sense of control and power — anorexia nervosa. It became my new "best friend" and allowed me to change the dynamics with my family, friends, and girlfriend.

Anorexia develops over time. It develops because of traumatic life experiences as well as emotional and psychological issues. It results from feelings of guilt, shame, worthlessness, low self-esteem, and the inability to exercise control over any part of your life. These feelings, however, do not occur in a vacuum. They develop based upon your relationships with other people, whether it be with parents, friends, romantic partners, and so forth. The very dynamic of these relationships, and often the dysfunction that accompanies them, can scar you permanently and affect your ability to form healthy relationships. In my case, I lived my life for everyone else, but never for me. I was technically alive but felt dead. Ultimately, anorexia saved me as much as it harmed me. As I now go through the recovery process, I have learned so many life lessons, all of which I am going to share with you, in the hope that I can help you down the path to true happiness and liberation.

Chapter Two

It Takes a Village

My journey towards anorexia developed, in large part, from my disillusionment with people. It started when I was young and stretched through my time in college and law school, my legal career, and my romantic relationships. For me, the statement that "people suck" was, and sometimes still is, a very accurate sentiment. People gossip too much. They can be materialistic and selfish. Some have oversized egos, which, for me, is a gross turn off. Many have no common sense or emotional intelligence. Most are not good listeners and not good talkers either. I could go on and on, but there's no point.

Hillary Clinton was correct when she said that it takes a village to raise a child. It is so important that the community, through schools and other institutions, complement the parent-child relationship in helping to shape the character, values, and abilities of our young people. One of the important influences on a child — and on society generally — is organized religion. When I was young, my parents sent me to a Catholic grammar school, and later a Catholic high school. They did so because they believed, correctly, that I would receive a better education.

It wasn't the education that was the problem. It was the indoctrination. In Catholic school, they care as much about your moral values as they do about the quality of instruction you are receiving. Morality co-exists with intellectual pursuits, as if they are inextricably linked. I remember my grammar school days well. At specific Catholic events, like the May Crowning, our class would serve as the "choir" for the mass, singing songs that still remain unfamiliar to me. Each month, each of us would have to go to confession, where we would enter this little room with the priest behind a wall so that we could not see him. We were required to start out by saying, "bless me, father, for I have sinned, since my last confession I have ......" and then list all of the "sins" we had committed. After hearing our misdeeds, the priest would command us to say a prayer, like the Hail Mary, twenty-five times. I'm not sure how he arrived at the number. Of course, religion class was also part of our curriculum. We would read passages from the bible and they would be interpreted for us, for the purpose of giving us yet another overarching moral principle to guide our actions. Of course, we all had to know the Ten Commandments, and were taught about the Stations of the Cross.

To me, none of this made sense. I didn't understand any of the methods of the Catholic education. First, I felt even then that we were all being bunched together like faceless human beings. We all had to fit neatly into this nice little box of morality. Everything was black and white, simple and easy. The answers were already there for us, so there was no need to ask any questions. We just needed to accept everything we were told. Now, if any student did have questions, and the teacher or priest didn't know the answer, we would be told to have "faith" in God and trust Him in His ways. So, if we asked how God could let the holocaust happen, we would be told that "God works in mysterious ways." In other words, don't ask questions. Stay within the little moral box that we constructed for you even before you were born. There is no "I" in Catholicism; there is only "we." Individuality, introspection, self-development, creativity, complexity, and grayness were all antithetical to the Catholic regime. It was designed to crush the human spirit. So if I asked myself "who is Adam," the answer would be "you are just like everyone else."

The problem is that it wasn't true. It didn't reflect or respect the unique and wonderful differences that each individual should celebrate in their own lives. It didn't allow people to define happiness and meaning on their own terms and find liberation and peace by expressing their authentic selves, free from some ridiculous, self-serving construction of the world that tried to suppress human freedom. Perhaps the best example of this is my brother Christopher, who is a homosexual. I discovered that my brother was gay when I was twelve years old. My parents already knew and, I must say, they were always supportive and unconditionally accepting and loving of him as their son. As someone who had a Catholic upbringing and attended a Catholic high school, it must have been agonizing for him to deal with his sexuality while the Church was calling it an abomination against God. I didn't realize the hell it must have been for him. In fact, my brother eventually left the Catholic Church, as they had told him he wasn't welcome there. He began attending a non-denominational service with his partner. From that point on, my hatred of Catholicism was born, and it grew every time that I heard the Church condemn homosexuality. I always felt that God loves everyone not for who they are, but how they treat other people. The Catholic Church's condemnation of certain groups is just the opposite of what God stands for, and I believe God would look with disfavor upon Catholicism. Now that the pedophilia scandal has been uncovered, I cannot believe how any priest can stand up and preach about morality. The Catholic Church is perhaps the best example of immorality.

The Church damaged and suppressed both my brother and me. I was twelve years old and had no emotional or spiritual development. No sense of self and self-awareness. As I look back, what bothers me is how these people actually believe that they have the answers to life's most difficult questions. Questions about the universe, an afterlife, and what happens when we die are so complicated, and perhaps beyond our reasoning capabilities, that any claim by the church to have answers is unjustifiable. To make matters worse, the Church forces upon everyone a cookie-cutter moral code that has ruined people's lives. My brother suffered. Others who are gay may suppress their sexuality. Those who have been taught that divorce is immoral may stay in terrible marriages. The list goes on and on. The Church is not about acceptance or embracing diversity. It is about rejection, negativity, and self-sacrifice.

I defined myself according to the definitions, answers, and expectations that were provided by the village — schools, the Church, my friends, and neighbors. So who was I at twelve? I was a people pleaser who lived in fear. I just wanted everyone to like me and approve of me. In 1989, that defined my existence. I had questions and I didn't like the answers that I was provided with. Then I went to a high school.

Chapter Three

High School and My First Relationship — Welcome to My World

I was thirteen years old when I enrolled at a Catholic high school close to my New Jersey hometown. My parents sent me there because the school had an excellent reputation. My freshman and sophomore year were more of the same: church services, confessions, and conformity. I was used to it and it didn't bother me. However, I was just going through the motions. Honestly, I was not rejecting the notion of God or an afterlife. I was just looking with disdain upon those who claimed that they were representative of His message. Nothing could be further from the truth or Truth. There was one difference, though — I was starting to rebel. I would fuck up in class, not do my homework, perform poorly on my tests, and otherwise not care about my education. I received twelve detentions that year, which the school called "JUG," meaning "Justice under God." This was the first time I refused to conform. I was breaking away even though I wasn't consciously aware of it yet. I just thought the whole system was bullshit. So I did the things that I found enjoyable. I hung out with my friends and started drinking alcohol in my sophomore year, listened to Metallica and Iron Maiden, played baseball, and just had fun. For the first time in my life, I didn't care if I got in trouble or garnered criticism. I wish I would have carried this demeanor throughout my teenage and adult years. Unfortunately, it would be short lived. I think that's because I wasn't rebelling against the people; I was rebelling against the morality and simplicity. I was trying to develop an identity. I wanted to go against the norm, do something aberrational that would speak loudly and clearly to the world, saying that I was different and nobody could do anything to get me back inside the box.

I got that chance, and took full advantage of it, during the summer after my sophomore year. When I was fifteen years old, along with one other player on my high school baseball team, I had the opportunity to travel to Belgium and represent the United States in an international competition with teams of a similar age. Overall, it was a very enjoyable experience. Playing baseball wasn't even the best part. It was my first time in Europe. We could drink as much as we wanted. We did just that, and got drunk almost every night. You could go to "peep shows" where you sat behind a window while a girl engaged in sexual activity. I was also introduced to the red light district, where prostitutes stood in front of a window and you could literally window shop to find the perfect girl with whom to have intercourse. My friends took full advantage of this service. For me, I just couldn't do it. I was shy — and a virgin.

In any event, one night when we were at a bar, I noticed a very pretty woman named Natalie, and, in a move very unlike me, I approached her and asked if she wanted a drink. She hardly spoke English, so I had to make some hand gestures to convey my intentions. Of course, it was fairly obvious, so the language barrier was not problematic. Thereafter, we sat down with our drinks and talked in the best manner that we could. What I gleaned from the conversation was that she was twenty-two years old and living in Belgium, but had always had the dream to move to the United States, get a college degree, and become a nurse. Things were going well in this conversation; I liked her and she liked me. She then asked how old I was. Instead of saying fifteen, which in my opinion would have ruined my chances of going any further with this girl, I lied and said I was twenty-one. I looked like I was about fourteen, but I had a fake ID.

After about an hour, we went for a walk and began to kiss each other passionately. I became terrified at the prospect of having sex. If you had told me that I would lose my virginity at fifteen in a small town in Belgium, I would have laughed. This was, however, no laughing matter. I was certain that I was probably going to screw it up and give a miserable performance. Shit, I didn't even know how to put on a condom! To make matters worse, we were leaving to go back home in two days, so Natalie probably thought that we should get this thing going as soon as possible. Well, I got lucky. After messing around for about twenty minutes, she, in terribly broken English, asked me to meet her at the bar the next night. Of course I said yes, and I knew what that yes meant. We were going to have sex and I was going to lose my virginity. I had never been more anxious and nervous at the same time.

From sunrise to sunset the next day, I was petrified. Every thought imaginable went through my head. Will she like me? Am I going to please her? I was so worried about pleasing her that I did not spend even one moment thinking about myself, my needs, and my expectations. The "people pleaser" was in full force, and Natalie had the control. So, later that night, I lost my virginity. How was the sex? It was about what you would expect from someone who had never done it before. It was made better by the fact that she was experienced and compensated for my shortcomings. In the end, it was pleasurable for the both of us. By the next morning, as we said goodbye, she hugged me and said how much she always dreamed of coming to the United States. Well, you won't believe what happened next.

She came to see me about eight months later. Then it was time for the truth to make an appearance. The first thing I had to tell her was that I was not twenty-one years old. I was a fifteen-year-old high school student, and I'd been a virgin when she'd met me. To my surprise, she didn't react as negatively as I thought she would. I did, of course, apologize and explain that I really liked her and thought that if she knew my age, she would not have wanted to become involved with me. She seemed to understand. So she was now in the United States and living in my parents' house for the duration of her stay. Basically, I would go out drinking with my high school buddies, she would explore New York City and all of the other places that she always wanted to see, I would come home drunk, and we'd sometimes have sex. I would realize later how selfish and hurtful that was because she was hoping that we would have a relationship. I was just interested in the physical intimacy. It's funny to look back and realize that you made a mistake that you didn't realize was a mistake at the time. Do you apologize? I did. When I hurt someone's feelings, intentionally or not, I feel terrible.

My parents knew that Natalie wanted to stay in the U.S. and go to school. So guess what? They eventually offered to keep Natalie in our house for an extended and indefinite period of time. To say the least, I was shocked at this idea. I could not fathom that this girl, who I'd known for two days in Belgium, would now be living in my house. So, did I speak up and voice my objections? Of course not. I acted as if I was pleased at this news, and smiled and hugged her. Once again, I betrayed my feelings, betrayed myself, and just let the situation happen. I didn't use my voice. In fact, by not saying anything, I said everything. The truth is, I was afraid to hurt Natalie and was willing to hurt myself to avoid causing her pain. I felt like such a loser. If I could not stand up to this, I might never be able to stand up for anything, or have healthy control over anything.

Ultimately, Natalie stayed in the house for several years, and our physical relationship turned into a friendship. However, during those earlier days, things were difficult. Whenever I brought a date into the house to meet my parents, she got angry. Whenever I went out with my friends but did not include her, she got upset. It was as if I had the obligation to include her and bring her to every function or event I was attending. I was furious, but felt that nobody really understood why I was so angry. I felt that no one respected the fact that I wanted to have my own life, just as it was before the Belgium trip. I desperately wanted some measure of healthy respect, control, and validation. I felt like she just moved into my house and I got kicked out. Honestly, though, part or most of the problem was that I never expressed these feelings to my parents. I didn't want to create negativity or hurt anyone. So I did what I was accustomed to doing — nothing.

After the Natalie fiasco, I was angry. I'm not really sure why I was so angry. No one really did anything to hurt me — neither my parents nor Natalie. It didn't matter, though, because my anger wasn't logical. For once, instead of directing it inward, I wanted to pretend like I had been a victim of some injustice. I no longer cared about people respecting me at this point. I just wanted to do something that would represent the ultimate "fuck you" to anyone and everyone who was making me feel invisible and unimportant. I wasn't going to go out, however, and mess around with some random girl. I wanted to break boundaries. I wanted to have a relationship with someone regardless of their age, marital status, or race. I just wanted to have an experience that was a pure expression of me, or that brought something out of me that I never knew existed. For me, expressing myself creatively would allow my voice to shine. If the real Adam couldn't say something, then he could at the very least do something. This whole "fuck you" project seemed to me like a pipe dream, but it soon became a stunning reality.

When I was sixteen, I worked at a small coffee shop in my hometown. I saw the same people every day, gave my token smile, and engaged in my bullshit small talk. There was one stunningly attractive woman who started to come in regularly. I could tell that she was significantly older than me. I also noticed, by virtue of the diamond ring on her left hand, that she was married. That, however, didn't stop me. Ultimately, it didn't stop either of us. She was just so pretty. Yikes. Beauty as a moral justification.

Slowly, we began talking, mostly about trivial matters like the weather, where she lived, where she worked, and the like. She had moved to New Jersey three years earlier from Seattle, so we discussed how she'd handled the adjustment, what she liked about the northeast, and what she thought of the people. I learned that she had two children and had been married for several years. We also talked about other banal things, partly because, I think, we were both afraid to test the waters and see if these burgeoning feelings were real. I mean, we only saw each other in the coffee shop. Yet things were beginning to escalate. Our conversations became deeper. We looked at each other differently. She inquired about my age, as I did hers. As I'd surmised, she was older — twenty-five years older. I didn't care. I was looking for something to make me feel wanted. I wanted to feel needed and, dare I say, loved. Heck, *liked* would have been fine too. The point is, I wanted affection based on something real. I wasn't quite sure, consciously or subconsciously, if I cared if it came from a married woman, an elephant, or an object.

What I do know is that, as our relationship evolved, the values and morals that I thought were once part of my character instantaneously vanished. I gave her my phone number if she ever "wanted to talk." She called me one day and asked me to meet her at a park about three blocks from the coffee shop. So we met at the park and talked on a slightly more intimate level. She talked about how her marriage hadn't really been a marriage for the last couple of years. Her husband was emotionally devoid. I should have told her that my life hadn't really been a life for the past sixteen years, so she should consider herself not so unfortunate. That was, however, way too silly. I did have a life, but I wasn't living it authentically. Or maybe I should have been more assertive and said, "Why are you still in the relationship?" I really didn't care or know what to say. Someone twenty-five years older than me was discussing intimate details of her marriage. She trusted me. She smiled at me. I felt like I was living in a new world. This person seemed to like the authentic me. I wanted to freeze that moment in time because I was afraid that it might go away in an instant. It didn't. During our conversation I touched her hand. It was one of those moments where the physical touching was inconsequential, but the emotional bond undeniable.

I felt weird. I went into my default mode of thinking. I felt a sense of shame and self-hatred because I had just engaged in a morally repugnant act — I'd made a romantic gesture to a married woman with two children. I was sixteen years old and she was forty-one. What kind of person was I? What kind of person was she? At that moment, part of me was hoping that the park incident would end at that simple gesture, and that things would return to normal. The other part of me was hoping that this was just the beginning of something that was going to take me places that I had never been before.

For the first time, my conscience was taking a back seat to pure hedonism, and whether morally repugnant or not, against the Ten Commandments or not, I couldn't escape the feeling that I didn't care. Don't get me wrong — I cared that I didn't care, but my feelings were what they were. For the first time, my concept of morality began to get more complex, more gray, and more difficult to grasp. I don't know if this was self-serving, or just a more mature assessment of the circumstances. Should people stay in unhappy relationships? If they do stay, is it ok to have an affair with someone who brings them true happiness? I had the questions, but no answers. This was not a time for answers; it was a time for action.

So, as I became a senior in high school and began to contemplate my life thereafter, we began to see each other on a more regular basis. This was, perhaps, the most regrettable experience in my childhood, although at the time I thought it was a gift from the Almighty. I was sixteen years old, and I was on the threshold of being in an extra-marital affair. Our brief meetings continued for a short while, until she eventually suggested that we meet in more secluded places so that we could talk without fear of being noticed. As I got closer to seventeen, my thoughts were on having sex with her and whatever else, but I wasn't sure of her intentions. All of these concerns dissipated when we kissed. I'll never forget it — I was so excited. The experience left me paralyzed with so many different emotions. Was I a bad person for doing this? Was I less culpable because she had initiated the contact? I didn't know what to make of the situation. It was making me, though and, more importantly, it was starting to control me.

Thereafter, she would ask me to come to her house on various days of the week when her husband was at work. It started to become a routine exercise. I would go to her house, we would fool around, we would talk for a while, and I would leave. As I look back, I think that I was filled with contradictory, almost irreconcilable feelings. At no point in our affair did I feel comfortable or proud of what I was doing. I didn't even know why I did it. Maybe it was because I needed the love and affection. Maybe it was just for pleasure. I think the real reason was that it empowered me. I was sixteen, messing around with this woman, and not many people could say that they had ever done that. So it made me feel special, important, and loveable. She filled my emotional void. It didn't matter that the affair was immoral. It didn't matter that if her husband found out he would be devastated. I had finally experienced validation. I finally allowed myself to take the mask off so I could be seen. My worst fear actually became my happiest moment.

I finally had a legitimate reason to feel good about myself. I thought that I had a certain degree of control over my life, because I could see her at predictable times and continue our intimate relationship. Now, I still felt those feelings of shame and guilt, but I went into self-denial, because, besides my mom and dad, this was one of the first times that someone liked my authentic self. I didn't want to pollute that feeling with negative energy. So the affair continued up until I had to leave for college. For about two years during college, we would sometimes hook up when I returned home for the holidays. Eventually, the affair ended, due mostly to the fact that I had a girlfriend, and she gracefully understood that, as a young adult, it was time for me to move on with my life. We talked for a few years, but we don't communicate anymore.

Chapter Four

The College Years: Suspicious Minds

After high school, it was time to select the college of my choice. My parents gave me carte blanche to choose whatever college I wanted to attend. What did I do? I picked the university as far away as possible from my hometown. I wanted to get away from my life, my friends, my ex-girlfriends, and my environment. I wanted the chance to meet people who knew nothing about me, and with whom I had a clean slate. What I truly wanted to do was run away from my feelings. I would learn very soon that this was not possible.

In 1993, I enrolled at the University of Southern California. The campus was so beautiful, with flowers surrounding the stunning architecture of its buildings. There was a sense of youthfulness, a sense of vibrancy that made me feel like I was starting my life all over again. There were approximately 35,000 people at USC, and I didn't know a single person. I liked it that way. Sometimes, anonymity is better than notoriety. You have a second chance to make a first impression, a new opportunity to create your own reputation. I didn't know what I wanted to be or to say. I just wanted it to be authentic.

When I first arrived in Los Angeles, it was like a whirlwind of confusion. There were so many diverse people everywhere. Student groups were lined up all across the campus (which was massive), and there were thousands of freshmen wandering around aimlessly trying to figure out where they were living, where they could enroll in courses, and where they had to purchase their books. It was chaos with a sense of logic. When I first moved into my dormitory, there were upper-level college students waiting outside to help bring our belongings to our respective dorm rooms. They seemed pleasant and welcoming, and it was nice, even on a superficial level, to meet someone who was a student at USC. There was, of course, a method to this madness. When my stuff was brought into my dorm room, one of the guys said "Adam, come by our fraternity house tonight, we're having a kickass party." Now things started to make sense: the guys that were helping people move in were doing so to identify the people they wanted to pledge their fraternity. And I fell right into the trap. It really wasn't a trap *per se* because these were nice people, but my associations were being made even before I knew it.

So I went to the fraternity house that night, got drunk, and had a great time. It was fun; I had just flown in from New Jersey and all of a sudden I was surrounded by people who were being so nice to me! I had almost instantly made friends! I felt liberated, empowered, and important. I felt like those people liked me unconditionally. I immediately felt as if I had made the right decision to travel across the country. I could reinvent myself, and maybe that would allow me to reinvent the feelings that I harbored against myself. I wanted to be born again. I was excited and decided to become a pledge in their fraternity. I was excited to be Adam.

To my utter dismay, the negative feelings I thought I had run away from came quickly roaring back. As a pledge in the fraternity, there was, of course, some hazing, which I hated because it was de-humanizing and plain wrong to treat people in that manner. To its credit, this fraternity did not haze us nearly as much as some of the others, and I had some wonderful and memorable times. That wasn't the aspect which bothered me — what screwed with my feeble mind was the fact that, after traveling 3,000 miles from home, I found myself in the same position I'd been when I was younger — I was being controlled by other people. I came here to get away from that, not to get involved in it again. As a pledge, I was under the control of the members of that fraternity. Now, there is nothing inherently wrong with that. It didn't matter to every other pledge, but, given my history, it brought back terrible memories. What made matters worse was that I had created this reality. I chose this path after just days in college. I should have known better. The feelings of self-hatred paid me another visit — and this time they were here to stay. I was a stranger in a strange world, but on the inside things were more familiar than ever.

In response to this, I said goodbye to Adam and I created the image again. If I hated so much of what was on the inside, then I desperately needed to gain approval for what was on the outside. In other words, the problem was not with my fraternity "brothers." The problem was with me. I was never content to be me; instead, I created an image of myself that I thought everyone would like. I wanted to portray myself as an outgoing, "cool" person that loved to party, get drunk, and do whatever else. I wanted desperately to be liked and was willing to do almost anything to gain approval. So, I never disagreed with anyone or anything. For me image wasn't everything — it was the only thing. I came to USC to make a change in my life. What I did was create precisely the same existence that I left behind.

During my freshman year I also met Erica, a girl from California who lived on the same floor in my dormitory. She was strikingly pretty and had a glowing personality. We initially became friends, but there was an unspoken chemistry between us, and as time went by we were able to share many of our most intimate thoughts with each other, whether they were family problems, issues of insecurity, feelings of low self-esteem, or more existential questions like what we would like to do with our lives. At that time, Erica was dealing with relationships that had both ended and were beginning. Prior to enrolling at USC, she had been dating someone who served in the Navy. She really did like him, and I listened as she talked about the experiences they had together. At this point, my feelings for her were in between friendship and romance, but the uncertainty of my feelings at that point made it palatable to discuss her romantic situation. She then told me that she had recently broken up with him and was dating someone new who was coming in for the weekend to visit. Shockingly, she had the audacity to ask if they could use my bedroom because he wouldn't be able to sleep on the girls' side of the dorm. Of course, "people pleaser" Adam said yes. What bothered me the most was that it was such a knee-jerk yes — it was not even remotely the product of deliberation or contemplation. I think maybe when someone takes you off guard in a situation, you subconsciously revert back to those old, ingrained behaviors that have dominated your life up to that point. My default-mechanism was to say yes to everyone and no to myself.

However, her boyfriend never came. Why? Well, we had sex about two days later. The sex was nothing to brag about, but it was nice because it wasn't just sex; it was intimacy between two people who genuinely liked each other. We'd only known each other for weeks, so I'm not sure if we really liked each other, or if it was just a connection based on familiarity to each other in an unfamiliar environment. In any event, I didn't know if I wanted a serious relationship with her, but it was nice to lie next to someone who cared about me and knew nothing about who I was or where I came from.

The following weeks solidified that we were, in fact, dating, and it was becoming serious. The Resident Advisor in my dormitory — with whom I became good friends — predicted that Erica and I would last three weeks together. Well, we lasted almost four years, nearly to graduation. During that time, we shared some wonderful moments, but I would more aptly characterize it as *she* had many wonderful moments. I did everything I could to make her happy. Whatever she wanted to do, we did. Wherever she wanted to go, we went. Not to sound egotistical, but I was the perfect "people pleaser" boyfriend. There is nothing I wouldn't or didn't do for Erica during those years. On her birthday, I bought her the most expensive jewelry that I could afford. Whenever she went to see her parents, I would fly there with her, even though I am terrified of flying. Whenever she wanted to shop for clothes, I would go with her. When she would come out of the dressing room and ask if a particular outfit looked good on her, I would lie and say yes so that we could get the heck out of there. I loved her as best I could. I pleased her in every way I could. I gave all of my power and control to her. Erica was never selfish or critical. I really did love her. Unfortunately, though, I didn't love myself while I loved her, and that made the love in our relationship toxic.

Over time, Erica felt that vibe. While I was emotionally present during the first year or so in the relationship, I began to pull away. I was still "there" but I was gone. We were still intimate and shared good times, but the innocence of the relationship was lost. I became angry at her and filled with resentment. Of course, the anger and resentment was really directed at me for not being myself during the relationship, and the relationship slowly began to deteriorate.

So what did she do? Three years after we began dating she cheated on me. I remember it like it was yesterday. I was supposed to meet her that night at the fraternity house, and we were going to get drinks or something. She was late. And as time went by, I became more worried. I was sitting on the front steps of my fraternity and thinking of any possible danger that she may be in, or any other circumstance that may have placed her in harm's way. Unfortunately, that was not the case. After about an hour of waiting, Erica arrived. I can't explain it, but I had an instinct that she had cheated on me. I hoped I was wrong. When I saw her, though, I knew I was right. When a girl has just finished having sex, there is a certain look on her face that lets you know. Erica had that look. I knew it and she knew I knew it. But my worthless self just played it off, and she later went home, and I got drunk. I didn't even have the courage to tell her how much she hurt me, how betrayed I felt at that moment, and how insensitive she was to do such a thing. I said nothing. I should have told her to fuck off. Instead, I smiled. I went into denial thinking that I must be wrong because *she would never do that to me*. Well, she did do that to me, and no matter how hard I tried, I couldn't escape the truth — the whole truth, which was that she was in control and had all of the power.

Over the next year we stayed together. Things were going reasonably well. That summer, I decided to go home to New Jersey, and she stayed with her parents in California. I later learned that she cheated on me again, with a different guy. Numerous times. How did I know? She told me. Was I hurt? Yes. Surprised? Yes and no. She had cheated on me twice, and if there was ever a point for me to walk away, it was now. Well, as embarrassed as I am to say this, I didn't. I thought I could save the relationship. I thought of all of the wonderful things I could do in our last year at USC to win her back. I would buy her anything, take her anywhere, but most importantly, treat her like a queen. It's at this point that other people thought I was nuts. It's like those horror movies, where the girl who is chased by the ax murderer goes into her car to get away and the car doesn't start. The audience, familiar with this scene, sighs in disbelief at the predictable ridiculousness. Well, the shit that I was putting up with made the people around me start reacting in the same way. I was the idiot whose car wouldn't start.

Anyway, my relationship-saving efforts worked. I got what I wanted. Our relationship got stronger. It got better not because I used my voice or exercised control over the situation. It got better because I did precisely those things that I knew she would love — I was again the "people pleaser." I was "home" again and, deep inside, my self-hatred grew.

For the first time, though, the "people pleaser" was now broken. For reasons that may or may not have had anything to do with voice, control, self-respect, or self-esteem, I began to lose interest in Erica. I hated what she had done to me. I spent all of our time together desperately seeking approval, yet, at the end I felt betrayed. I began to lose respect for her. And she knew it. I knew that I was in an unhealthy situation. I didn't want to be with someone who said she loved me while having sex with somebody else. My waning interest didn't make me feel empowered, but it did allow me to shed the subservient dynamic that I had brought into our relationship. At the very least now, I could start over. The thing is, though, I couldn't start over from the same place. If I did, I would have the same result. I needed a new "place," but, ultimately, that depended on whether I was presenting the image or the real person.

I was supposed to start over when I first went to USC, but I was time-delayed by about four years. Now that I saw the light about my circumstances with Erica, I was running towards it — without her. Suddenly, the situation then reversed itself. When I ran away, she started running back. She did everything she could do to get me back, but I refused, and moved on. It wasn't simply about exercising my voice and standing up for myself. It was about taking control of the situation, letting the girl know that, while I was a people pleasing freak, I wasn't going to let her take advantage of it any longer. I was repulsed by her for betraying me. It was over. Moving on was precisely what I needed to do. I didn't understand why it had taken so much shit to happen before I made that decision. I was happy that I had finally drawn a boundary with her, but that line should have been drawn two years earlier. I still had so much work to do, but I didn't know exactly what work needed to be done and I wondered who would help me uncover the reasons why my insecurities and inadequacies were penetrating every one of my relationships.

Ultimately, I made the decision to graduate in four-and-a-half years, because it made my course work less burdensome and I could take fun classes such as "Communication and Major Motion Pictures." Ha. The easiest "A" I ever achieved. I mean, do they make these classes on purpose? Do they really think that anyone in a college atmosphere will benefit from seeing movies like *The Graduate*? The only thing I learned was how much I would have loved to screw Anne Bancroft when she was at the height of her beauty. During this time, I really had an uptick with my frat buddies, probably because I would soon be graduating, and that conferred an unspoken level of seniority. Sure, my friends liked me. They thought I was cool, and I liked to hang out with them, go drinking, and have fun.

What they didn't, or couldn't, know was that inside of me the self-hatred, feelings of shame, guilt, and anger were almost to a boiling point. I hated the way Erica treated me, or to put it more accurately, how I had let her treat me. My frat buddies did not like me for who I was because I never showed them my authentic self. They liked me because of the image I projected. I would go drinking and basically adopt patterns of behavior so I would be "liked." That only fueled my self-hatred. I felt weak. I had no courage to be my true self and trust that I might attract people who liked me just the way that I was. The real problem I was facing, though, had nothing to do with Erica or my friends. Even in happy times, I still harbored feelings of self-loathing. I didn't understand. What was the source of this? It was as if I had an acute condition that could not be traced to anything physical or metaphysical.

So what did I do with all of these feelings? I started drinking incessantly. I drank every night, all the time, alone in my room. I love horror movies, so a typical night would be renting a movie like *Friday the 13th*, drinking twelve beers, running out to get fast food, and then passing out. Alcohol erased my problems. What I needed, though, was just the opposite. I needed my problems to erase the alcohol. If I just got over the self-hatred, if I just learned to accept and love myself, then maybe, just maybe, it would be ok. But that didn't happen, and it was a harbinger of something to come — anorexia — the struggle of my life.

Chapter Five

The Law School Years

Trapped in a World That's Troubled with Pain

If there are two things that I could identify as ultimately leading to my eating disorder, the first would be that I had no control over a reality that had become intolerable. This reality was intolerable for one major reason: all of the things that I dreamed of and which gave me great optimism and inspiration, whether it was the prospect of being a great lawyer, or meeting my future wife, turned out to be mere fabrications.

This all began in law school, which immediately followed my graduation from college. It was 1998. When I went to law school, I despised lawyer jokes. Now, I understand why they exist. When you walk in front of a law school, any law school, there are these beautiful statements saying things akin to "in the service of others," "making positive change on people's lives," "equal justice and due process for all," and so forth. It made me feel so optimistic about the law. I wanted to accomplish social change, defend the innocent, and protect the "underdog." I wanted to be a lawyer for all of the reasons that always defined my character. I wanted to do "justice" in the profession. I wanted to give a voice to those people who had none — the poor, disenfranchised, and disempowered. I wanted to be a resource for people when they needed help. I wanted to "right" all the "wrongs" in the world. I was truly an idealist, and I was determined not to sacrifice that value.

The problem is that those wonderful sentiments pretty much disappear the second you walk through the doors. Law school crushes idealism fairly quickly. It's funny because, not too long ago, I read something by an attorney who said that squashing idealism is one of the first things that happens during your first year. I'm not so sure that it happens that quickly, but it does happen. I'm not going to condemn law school, but I do believe it can be — and should be — so much more than it is now.

So many things I found intolerable in law school, and later, in the legal profession. First, law students are a strange bunch of people. In all fairness, there are wonderful people with whom I have formed good friendships, but, having said that, law students can be some of the most arrogant and egotistical people you will ever meet. Indeed, some of the people that I met as a law student were so stuck up they made me nauseous. I never quite understood why they had such a grandiose self-opinion. After all, who the fuck did they think they were? They were young law students who knew nothing whatsoever about the law and probably even less about life. Even if they were brilliant (which they were not), had they ever heard of the virtue of being humble? Eventually I felt bad for them because they were so pathetic. All they did was talk incessantly about themselves. It's funny, because the more highly they thought of themselves, the lower they were regarded by the more humble students. By acting the way they did, these idiots received the opposite reaction (scorn) than the one they had so desperately sought (admiration).

The second thing that sucks about law students is that they gossip and betray confidences. I cannot tell you how many times people would tell me about what someone else had said or done, who'd had sex with whom, what grade someone received on an examination, who'd been rejected from a firm, who'd been ridiculed in class, and whatever else. It was sad. I hate people who gossip. People love to talk about other people's lives, especially their weaknesses, more than they like to confront their own issues. It is a sign of immaturity and insensitivity. These are the reasons that I didn't enjoy law school. It was full of the people that I despised.

I also felt that the approach to law teaching could have inspired us to retain idealism and work to make the world a better place. In law school, you rarely hear people talk about values, the need to help people vindicate their rights before a court of law, the important task of assisting indigent people in having their rights heard in court, and the need to defend people who are charged with crimes by overzealous prosecutors. You don't hear about how the law itself can be an important vehicle for social change and that every student in that classroom can have a role in that change. Law professors don't tell their students to pursue their passions in life and fight for what they believe in. Instead, you incessantly read case after boring case, wondering how the hell this even relates to law, its practice, or even life itself. Law school is a tremendous disappointment on a variety of levels. A major disappointment is that law school has nothing to do with the practice of law.

Perhaps the biggest realization is that the practice of law, for the most part, has nothing to do with helping people create a more meaningful and just world.

The truth is, being a law student, and a lawyer, is about money, not ideals. The administrations at most law schools focus on helping law students obtain employment at high-paying, private law firms. I am not saying this is wrong, but it's the reality. What is private practice? It's those firms where you get paid about $100,000 during your first year, and they work you to death until you feel like you'd rather be parking cars at a local restaurant than perusing 5,000 documents in connection with some worthless case. The sole job of a new lawyer in some of these big firms is to make the partners money. That's it. There are no other goals. They don't ordinarily care about helping people who can't pay their $400 per hour rates. Sure, law firms have "pro bono" requirements where they must represent indigent defendants, but those cases are often given to the most inexperienced attorneys in the firm.

What do law schools do? They push you in the direction of making money at the big firms. They don't tell you that you won't have a personal life. They don't tell you that you'll be working weekends. They don't tell you that a good number of lawyers at these firms are complete assholes. They don't tell you that the young lawyers you'll work with can be gossipy, back-stabbing pricks because they view you as an obstacle on their path up the corporate ladder. For those who want a different path, good luck. Law schools don't push you to be a public interest lawyer. A public defender. A lawyer for the ACLU. They don't advertise with any degree of regularity or intensity the types of jobs that serve the public welfare or public good. You get the picture. Placing their students in high-profile, private law firms increases the school's reputation and ranking. That matters more than a student's individual desire to "make a difference."

Ultimately, I spent three years in law school feeling alone in a world that didn't resemble what I hoped it would. From when I was twelve years old, I dreamed of being a lawyer. Sadly, the experience never matched the reality. Of course, I made friends and they didn't seem to mind it much at all. But for me, law school was all about learning how to serve other people. I didn't care about money. I still don't care about money. I didn't care about living in a nice house with a nice car. For me, life was — and still is — about people. It's about trying to use what you know to give back to the community. In law school, I felt like this was equivalent to speaking a different language.

So what did I do in response to the culture that I encountered? I made one of the worst mistakes in my life. I sold out for the money. I abandoned my idealism. I was twenty-six years old. I was in the top 15% of my class. All of my friends had secured jobs paying nearly $90,000 to start. Then there was me, hoping to be a public defender or a lawyer serving the public interest. I buckled under the pressure of being alone. So I betrayed everything that I stood for and agreed to work at one of these big firms with so many names on the front of its building that it would take a week to pronounce them all.

How did this start me down the path towards anorexia? Well, at that point in my life, I would describe myself as having been possessed of the following characteristics:

- Inability to use my voice and set boundaries
- Feelings of self-hatred and worthlessness
- Feeling like I had no control in my life
- Feelings of low-self-esteem
- Being a "people pleaser"
- Feeling alone in a world inconsistent with my values
- Spiritual and idealistic death

In my law school years, I had the ingredients. I began to feel like I didn't even know who I was and what I stood for anymore. I was beginning to lose control over myself, my life, and my happiness. The end of my idealism was the beginning of a long path towards self-destruction.

Chapter Six

The Law Firm Years

You Can't Shut Out the Truth

Let me say that the legal profession can be a noble, meaningful, and fulfilling calling. I know many wonderful lawyers who dedicate much time and energy to helping people and strive to make positive changes in their communities. The law itself can be an amazing agent for progressive reform in ways that make individuals' lives better. I know lawyers that conduct themselves with honesty, integrity, and with the very idealism that I had — and let go of — in law school. These are the lawyers that vindicate the values that the legal profession seeks to uphold and represent. Unfortunately, however, my experience as a lawyer was the opposite of what I envisioned it would be.

My experience as a lawyer started in 2001. Everything got off to a great start. I was always a talented writer and, in the legal profession, especially if you are a litigator, the vast majority of your time is spent writing. The partners in the firm immediately took a liking to me because I could write well, and they could therefore depend on me to complete complex assignments that were both important and time-consuming. I really didn't mind this, because I felt valued and respected. I would draft pleadings, motions, trial briefs, appellate briefs, mediation statements, and the like. I felt the firm liked me because of my true self and legal abilities. What I didn't know was that I was being liked by the wrong people for the wrong reasons.

Although I wouldn't have admitted it at the time, I was "people pleasing" at every turn. I was the child and they were the parents. I would stay as late as needed and come in early day after day, just to make them happy. The good reviews I received allowed me to rationalize the fact that I had sold out. I didn't have time for introspection because I was afraid of it. I knew that if I looked inside of myself even for a minute that I wouldn't see myself. I wouldn't see anything. I was a fraud. With every paycheck and compliment, I could steep in the denial that I was forcing myself into.

So I lived, almost unwittingly, the life of a fake person searching for fake compliments in a world that valued fake people and false idols. Being false, controlled, and trying to please other people came so naturally to me that I thought it *was* me. I remember reading *Twilight of the Idols* by Frederic Nietzsche, in which he brilliantly describes the downslide, and eventual destruction, of the Christian values that had ultimately come to dominate the masses. Nietzsche came to the realization that Christian morality was a crock of shit, that it was designed to give hope where none exists, and more importantly, that it was the granddaddy of nihilism. For Nietzsche, life was about living it to its fullest, harboring all aspects of your creative self into a superhuman force that transforms you and transcends time. Christian morality, with its emphasis on self-sacrifice and self-denial, was the poison that would destroy the pinnacle of human potential. I wasn't living that life. I was ordinary, common, and trite. I was a sophisticated hooker in a fancy suit.

I desperately wanted to become the original, creative, and transcendent person that Nietzsche described, but I was instead a flimsy kiss-ass with 226 pounds of fat on my body; any true attempt to appraise my life honestly would reveal the absurdity of my attempts to forget the shame and self-loathing that lived just under my skin. I couldn't handle such a reality check. I couldn't handle the fact that there was no way to escape from the truth of my choices. I was becoming what I never wanted to become. If I completed the process and became that person, then maybe I could never turn back. So what did I have? Nothing and everything. I still had my shame, self hate, and desire to make everyone around me feel happy. Little did I know that I had the respect of no one.

In my second year, and in those that followed, I came face to face with consequences of my decision, not because I was more astute but because it was so much more obvious. I was working all the time. I had almost no personal life. I again felt that other people were controlling my life. What really made me angry was that I didn't like the people that were exercising this control. The lawyers I worked with were strikingly similar to those with whom I went to law school. Just as it was in law school, the gossip in a law firm is like a quickly metastasizing cancer. There are few people you can trust, and if you think you can trust your "friends," think again. I cannot tell you how many times I revealed confidential information to those I thought I could trust, only to find out that other people soon knew this personal information. I was mortified. It didn't stop there.

Gossip isn't limited to truth. Other lawyers, especially those on your same level and who are theoretically in "competition" with you for promotions, will spread outright lies to others in the firm, whether it is about your work or personal life. Not only is this damaging to your reputation, it is humiliating because in a law firm, when one person gossips about another, it is only a matter of time before everyone knows the "secret," regardless of its veracity. It should come as no surprise to you that those I considered good, honest people within the firm resigned after a year or two.

In addition, it was not uncommon for the lawyers I worked with to take credit for the work I completed. When you work on a case, there is the partner/supervisor, normally followed by a senior associate and junior associate (me). Thus, for example, if the assignment is for a legal brief or memorandum, I will be responsible for drafting it and then submitting it to the senior associate for review. Well, I am a good writer, and I cannot tell you how many times I provided the senior associate with my work and she made no revisions whatsoever, yet brought it to our supervisor and claimed it as her work product. There was nothing I could do about it. What was I supposed to do? Complain? How was I going to prove it?

What I really, truly did not like about law practice was that if a partner or senior attorney did not like you, even if the reason was meritless, you could get fired or otherwise relegated to bullshit assignments. Power was the excuse for unjust and disgraceful behavior. I'm not going to say anymore, except that the saying "power is the greatest aphrodisiac" is true.

Perhaps the thing I hated most about practicing law was that it wasn't meaningful, purposeful, or fulfilling. I was not part of a practice that did justice, or helped the disempowered and disenfranchised. I was part of a materialistic culture that valued money and things, not people. Idealism had no place. Nowhere was this more evident than in the litigation process, namely, in the "billable hour" process. For example, when a medium or large-sized corporation gets sued for any reason, they retain a civil defense firm, somewhat like the firm at which I worked, to begin the litigation process. Lawyers charge by the hour, which can be extraordinarily expensive. Some lawyers charge $400 or more for each hour they spend on a project.

To put this in perspective, the litigation process is an extraordinarily long (it can take years), and tedious process. Both sides "paper" each other to death by, among other things, filing motions, requesting documents through discovery, conducting depositions, and making preparations for trial. Most cases, however, never make it to trial. They almost always settle. By this time, however, both sides can make hundreds of thousands of dollars (and maybe more). I was a part of this process many times. Not only did I feel like I was in a profession that was devoid of meaning and justice, but I felt like a cog in a wheel. I had betrayed my values. I felt like a worthless human being because I was a worthless human being. For me, being a lawyer was such a terrible experience that I was unable to fake it anymore. I got fired from my first job. I got a second job and got fired from that one, too. I went to a third law firm and, after a few months, simply walked away. It was over. I was just as disillusioned with the law as I was with Catholicism.

As I look back, the fact I practiced law for as long as I did (five years) amazes me. There is one lesson that I ultimately learned from this experience, though, which was to never look back and regret the mistakes you make because at the time you made them, you were in a different place and doing the very best you could to do the right thing. As the song, "No Day but Today" from *Rent* says, "forget regret, or life is yours to miss." One of my problems was that I was making a lot of mistakes and thinking of that line from *Rent* far too often. Maybe I wasn't always living with regret, but I wasn't living truthfully. I wasn't moving forward. What I hadn't yet realized, through my childhood, college, law school, law practice, and romantic relationships, was that I was setting myself up for a situation where I would eventually have to exercise exclusive control over something. I just didn't know what it was yet. I would soon. Ultimately, when I look back on my experience in the legal profession, I can only think of two things. First, I should have pursued my passions. Second, it really hurt to find out that the profession was not anything close to what I hoped it would be, that it was, in fact, nearly the opposite.

I wish they would have told us the truth in law school.

Chapter Seven

The Second Affair with a Married Woman

Reason Can't Stand In for Feeling

I miss Elvis Presley every day, even though I never knew him. He died when I was less than two years old, and I discovered his music when I was twenty-six years old. Prior to that, I hadn't thought much about Elvis; all I knew were the unfortunate details surrounding his death. The drug use, the difficulties he faced, and the isolated life that he lived. For some reason, I went into a Barnes and Noble store one day and purchased *Elvis: The Hits* and started playing it in my car. I enjoyed the music but I can't explain it; I saw a man behind the music.

There was something more to Elvis than just his music, and I wanted to find out what it was. So I bought more Elvis music and books by credible authors that detailed his life. I learned of a man not so different from myself. Elvis was troubled, looking for meaning in his life, trying to reconcile his fame with his authentic self, and, ultimately, trying to find peace in a life that no one but Elvis could imagine living. Before he performed at Madison Square Garden, I think Elvis summed it up beautifully when someone from the media asked a question and he said, "the image is one thing and the human being is another . . . it's very hard to live up to an image."[1] Yes, it is almost impossible.

During those unhappy days as a practicing lawyer, I had a second affair with a married woman, which still shakes me to this day. In 2003, I struck up a pleasant conversation with a woman I met when I was out with my friends, named Amy. She was very attractive and had a gorgeous body. It wasn't long before I was thinking how much I would like to have sex with her. I was also thinking, *Adam, there is no way she is going to mess around with a fat ass like you. She's probably shocked at your appearance.*

A few weeks later, I saw her at a local bar. She was wearing a black leather jacket, tight pants and, well, it turned me on within about forty-five seconds. To say the least, it was quite embarrassing to see her while in that state of arousal. My face turned red and I began to sweat and I prayed — *please God, make this go away.* I started thinking of the most disgusting images possible and then I pretended that I had an important, private phone call to make. It worked, and I luckily escaped the situation. But that was only the beginning. It is funny, though, that in these desperate and hopeless situations I find myself talking to the Almighty.

Anyway, we started talking again and I bought her a few drinks. I didn't know what to make of the whole thing, but the ever-present idealist in me (yes, there was a sliver left) was hoping against hope that she might be attracted to me and contemplating something more than friendship (or whatever we were doing). I did have this strange feeling that Amy might — just might — be attracted to me. Of course, this immediately hurled me into a dose of reality, thinking, *Adam, she'd rather hook up with an animal.* As we began to talk more openly about our lives, I found out that she was married with one child. Her husband had been born and raised in my hometown. She eventually wanted another child, but not for several years. She described how she loved her husband: he was a brilliant man who provided financial stability, was a great father, and a wonderful person. Talk about a buzz-killer. You should have seen my fake smile and head-nodding during this conversation. I did the best I could to show that I cared. I really did care, but not about her husband.

I almost laughed at myself. Here was Amy, married to a *brilliant* man who is a great father…and then there was me, a 226-pound fat guy talking to her, having sexual fantasies about her. I felt like a loser, not just for having those thoughts, but for what I felt I was as a person. I was a fat-ass with a drinking problem who sold out his own values for a job that he hated. Wow, I was certainly a catch, huh? I was a joke and I was completely aware of my standing in life. What I find interesting now is that, no matter how much weight I gained or alcohol I drank, I still believed I could hook up with the "hot" girls just like I had when I was eighty pounds lighter and equipped with a more sociable personality. I've noticed though, that people don't change their tastes no matter how or when their looks deteriorate. I think political correctness may have been born from one too many hurt feelings in a bar.

In any event, during our conversation, I didn't want my "please have sex with me" vibe to come out, in part because she was married with a child, but also because there was no way she would contemplate fooling around with a slob like me. Also, I had already been through the whole married woman affair thing and really didn't want to go through that again. I was, however, making one important miscalculation. There's more to life than logic. People don't necessarily make romantic decisions based upon how much you weigh or what job you have. Intimate and personal relationships are about feelings and, as Elvis said, reason can't stand in for feeling. I think this started to dawn on me when, in a drunken state, I asked her to have lunch with me. She said yes. I was shocked. Maybe she was also shocked that she said yes.

So we went to lunch the next weekend. I was nervous because I didn't know what the lunch meant. Was this a friendship thing or did she really have, for some crazy reason, an interest in me? That was a reflection of my own insecurities. Why did people want to be around me? I had no idea at that moment, but I didn't need any idea. I was going to find out soon. At lunch, we spent about a half hour with the typical small talk. I was prepared to stay at that level, because I wanted her to be comfortable, and I didn't want to do anything that might upset her. She was in control, not me.

After a few glasses of wine, however, Amy started going to places that made me uncomfortable. She began revealing to me that her relationship with her husband, while not necessarily bad, was not making her happy. Indeed, he was "brilliant," financially stable, and a wonderful father. However, the emotional and physical intimacy was not there. He was emotionally neglectful. She was missing the type of intimacy that really characterizes the essence of love. I wasn't sure if she thought that I might be able to supply it, or if she just wanted to have a moment of truth away from a mediocre existence.

I understood what she was saying, because I've always been a sensitive person who viewed pragmatism, practicality, and objective stability as a poor substitute for true love. I'd rather live in a shack with someone I love than in a mansion with someone with whom I can't connect on a deeper emotional level. She knew I understood that, or so it seemed. I was a good listener and she appreciated that. I was happy that she felt comfortable sharing such personal information. Eventually, we began to have lunch a couple of times a week. Sometimes we would just have fairly superficial discussions and other times it would be much more personal. It really didn't matter. We were enjoying being together. I was listening more than I was talking, but that was fine with me because, well, I didn't have much to say. I liked sitting there, looking at her, and re-discovering that there really is beauty in the world, in every way.

About two months after the innocuous lunches and pleasant conversations began, she asked me one day if I'd like to go with her to her dentist appointment. I was quite surprised but managed to mumble something indicating that I would like to do so. It was a cold winter night and, when we arrived at the dentist, she told me to wait in the car because her dentist knew her husband. Of course, I agreed. The problem was, it was about thirty-six degrees outside and I was stuck in a car with no heat for about forty minutes. When she finally came out, my feet were frozen but, of course, I told her that I was fine and had no problem waiting for her. What the hell was I supposed to say? *No, you made me freeze my ass off, fuck you.* Nope, can't say that. It's sort of like going on a date where the other person cooks dinner and then says, did you enjoy it? What are you supposed to say? *No, it was terrible. Your cooking sucks.* I really don't like when people ask me questions to which there is only one answer they want to hear, particularly when it forces me to lie.

After finishing her appointment, Amy drove her car outside the parking lot and, instead of making a right towards the highway, she pulled into a dark path that lead up to a beautiful golf course. When we stopped, I felt like Forrest Gump. I was staring straight ahead, my eyes wide open, with no idea what to say or do, and just simply scared out of my mind. I didn't know what was happening or what was going to happen, but I was immediately turned on. The problem this time was that there was no real way of hiding it. After what seemed like an hour, she grasped my hand and held it while we stared at each other. In a gesture that is so unlike me (I am quite shy), I pulled her towards me and we started kissing passionately for what seemed like forever. That was just the beginning. We did everything but have sex. The passion was so out of control that if a police officer was in the vicinity we would have probably been arrested. We touched each other and, if there hadn't been so many obstacles in the car, we would have had sex right there. Something started between us that blew my mind away. I was having intense feelings for her and could not believe the volatile nature of my emotions. It was as if I had finally found something that I had been searching for my entire life. I loved this girl (or so I thought), and all I wanted to do was be around her. We ultimately parted ways again. I was so over-stimulated that I was almost unable to sleep. I thought I was feeling what they meant by the term *happiness*. I had known her for years, and knew she was a good person. Maybe, after all, there could be some moral justification for what was happening, even if it seemed more subjective than the more objective immorality of the situation.

About a week later, her husband had to travel for work-related business. To my surprise, she invited me to come to her house that weekend. I had no idea what to expect. Would we talk? Have a drink? Kiss? Well, when I went to her house, we went into her living room, and she prepared us both a drink. I think it was cranberry-vodka but I don't remember because I was fixated on her body and how much I wanted to rip her clothes off at that very moment. Again, though, that voice inside me kept saying —*you're fat, she won't want to have sex with you.* Well, she did. As we were sitting on the couch talking, we started to kiss and do all the things that we did when we were by the golf course. This time, though, we had privacy and time. So, after about ten minutes of fooling around, we went upstairs to her room.

After it was over, I was speechless — literally. I had no idea what to say or how to act. I remember feeling that I had crossed the point of no return. I had now committed the immoral act of having sex with a married woman and I would never be able to change this fact. I wish better thoughts had been on my mind at the moment, but sometimes you can't control what goes on inside and outside of you. The truth is, though, it was more than sex. I liked who she was and what she brought out in me: honesty, innocence, hope, and optimism.

So, we went back down to her living room and I was still quiet, searching for the right thing to say. I felt bad. I felt shame. I felt guilt. Simultaneously though, I felt happy. I kept wondering, *maybe this is "immoral" according to some people's versions of morality, but it seems so right.* I mean, if someone is not happy in their marriage and finds true emotional intimacy with someone else, can that be wrong? Maybe it was both right and wrong. I was leaning, however, towards feeling like a bad person. They always say "it takes two to tango," but there's more to it than that. It would have taken only one of us to stop a situation that involved the potential to hurt others, including her husband and child. I was having these feelings as we were talking, as she was telling me how there was no fulfillment in her relationship with her husband, but that she felt the need to stay together for the sake of their child. Despite all the feelings going on inside me, and the conversation we were having, I blurted out, "Can we have sex again?" She looked at me with this mischievous smile, and said yes. So we had sex again. So much for my principles. I think inside I was starting to realize the "grey area" of the situation. It was even better this time. But when it was over — she said something that hit me to the core:

> *"Adam, you are really heavy, and you need to lose weight."*

I hated hearing that. I hated any mention of my weight. I still do to this day. I mean, can you please shut up about my weight?! Aren't there other things she could have said, like, "I really enjoyed being with you," or "I hope to see you soon?" No. She pointed at my stomach, which was so far extended that I couldn't see my feet or genitals without bending over. And she made it a point to touch my stomach. She made a lot of other comments about my weight too. Because of these criticisms, I began to experience those feelings of shame, guilt, and failure — the same as I did throughout my life. I started to feel that she, like everyone else, didn't like me unconditionally. I thought she would like me — or maybe love me — if I made certain changes. I didn't want to make changes. I never asked anyone else to change, and I didn't feel that they had that right either. Honestly, I have never been a judgmental person and I don't care what anyone else does to make their lives on this earth more tolerable. One thing I will never do is say the kind of things that Amy said to me. Maybe she was acting out of concern. Maybe I was way too sensitive. It doesn't matter. It was wrong. Let me take care of myself. I'm not going to criticize you for fucking around on your husband, so let's leave our little weaknesses out of the conversation.

It turned out that my relationship with her continued for the next four years. To this day, I can tell you that I loved her deeply and that she is a wonderful person. However, things turned out badly. She betrayed me and broke my heart. I thought love was enough to conquer all of the practical difficulties standing in the way of us being together. I was terribly wrong.

I have to say that our four-year affair was strange in many ways. A few days after fooling around near the golf course, Amy told me that she had just ended a two-year affair with another man. I was rather surprised when I heard this, because that meant that she was immediately going from one affair to another. My first thought was that her marriage must be terrible and devoid of love. My second thought, honestly, was that it was somewhat wrong to be having consecutive affairs. However, what really floored me is that, about a month into our affair, Amy's husband knew. He questioned her, and she admitted that we were seeing each other. The shocking part is that, for the next four years, he did nothing. He let it happen, in part, because he believed that Amy was going through a "phase" in her life. Eventually, he thought, Amy would come back and the marriage would stay intact. In the end, he was right.

For the duration of our affair, I was the textbook "people pleaser." I did everything possible that I could to make her happy and let her know that I loved her with all of my heart. There wasn't anything I wouldn't do for her. I really fell in love with her, and had hopes that maybe she would leave her husband someday and want to be with me. I not only loved her, but I felt sorry for her as well. She was in a difficult marriage that wasn't going to get any better, and the effects of a divorce on her children could be very damaging. So I tried to be the bright light that she could turn to during the day. Of course, I would get upset when I couldn't see or talk to her that much, and for many other reasons, but I never said a word. I didn't want to bring even a breath of negativity in a life that was already troubled and filled with doubt. I wanted her to associate me with happiness.

Unfortunately, though, that left me with no ability to express my feelings when I was sad, angry, hurt, depressed, or lonely. In many ways, I was alone in the relationship because I couldn't communicate with her like people do in normal, healthy relationships. Of course, that was because, by virtue of her being married, we were not in a healthy relationship. Indeed, it was difficult being the "other" person. I lived on her schedule at all times. We saw each other, talked on the phone together, ate together, had sex, and did whatever else together, on her terms and timetable. It didn't matter if she was available at times that were inconvenient for me. If I wanted the relationship to continue, I had to be available, or better stated, "on call," or we would never see each other. I was in familiar territory — in a relationship over which I had no control. I was replaying that pattern all over again. I never spoke up and said "no" to anything. I kept thinking in my mind, *Adam, why do you keep doing this?* I could never come up with an answer. I really had no idea. I knew that I loved her, but I also knew, in the back of my mind, that love might not be enough in the end.

After a couple of years, I began to notice the red flags signaling that she wasn't going to leave her husband. She sometimes talked about having a second child. She was going on more frequent vacations with her husband and child. She discussed buying a second home with her family. I should have started to distance myself, but I was starving for love and affection. I wanted to pretend that there was an alternative reality where Amy loved me unconditionally and I was free from all of the images and fabrications that I used to avoid those feelings of shame and inadequacy. Unfortunately, my fantasy bore no resemblance whatsoever to reality. She wasn't ever going to be with me. She wasn't going to give me what I needed or wanted. She wasn't going to be there for me when I needed her. She wasn't going to love me the way I deserved. Our affair was as close to a relationship as we would get. When I realized these things, I tried harder to please her and to do anything to make her happy. It was futile. She wasn't going to leave her husband. Yet, she wanted to continue the affair. So, at this point, the decision was mine. Do I end it? I should have. I didn't. I stayed despite all of the anger and resentment that was building up inside of me.

I did, however, pay a severe price. All of the negative, up-and-down emotions that I felt in the relationship, coupled with my unhappiness in the legal profession, became overwhelming. So one day I decided to stop feeling. I began abusing alcohol and drugs more than I had at any point in my life. Alcohol was easy. I drank every day after work and just went to sleep when I was tired. At first, illegal drugs were not appealing to me. They felt like a moral transgression. So I went to my doctor and gave a watered down version of my "anxiety" issues and existential problems. My doctor basically told me that he knew the cure to all of my worries: Valium. That's right. The wonder drug that would make my problems go away (at least in the dosage I planned to take). So after he mentioned that he would prescribe Valium, I played up my anxiety to such a level that he must have thought I was in need of urgent care. See, the more fucked up you seem, the more pills you get, the higher dosage you get, and most importantly, the more refills you get. Well, I won this battle. I got a prescription for Valium, 100 tablets, at 2 milligrams per tablet. This wasn't even the best part. I had three, yes, *three* refills.

I loved Valium immediately because it made me feel euphoric. When I combined it with alcohol (which I did on a daily basis) it made me feel happy, or at least some version of the emotion. The substance abuse resulted in part from the fact that I could not deal with the dynamics of my affair. I thought about Amy all the time. When I was awake, I would daydream about walking freely with her on a beach as the sun set on a beautiful Friday evening. I imagined us having a romantic dinner in New York, without any worry that someone or something would destroy the moment. I dreamt about making love to her inside, outside, everywhere, and nowhere. I don't know if these dreamy moments were cathartic or destructive. Sometimes I need to create fake worlds to escape my own existence. Of course, the substance abuse was about my much deeper emotional issues that still were not resolved and which had permeated my relationships, both in the legal profession and in my affair with Amy.

Substance abuse is only a temporary fix. Reality meant not being able to love Amy because love wasn't enough. Reality meant that eventually, the affair would be over. If I couldn't dream of another reality, I at least needed to escape this one. So I did, but this time things got worse. At first, I took Valium as it was prescribed. It took away my anxiety and made me feel euphoric. After a few days, I needed more. I wanted more. I started doubling my doses of Valium. In a few short weeks, I started taking triple the recommended dose. Within two months of getting the prescription, I was taking 20 milligrams of Valium per day. It was awesome. I didn't feel the pain anymore. Everyone else, though, saw the effects. The slurred speech. The dark circles under my eyes. The erratic behavior. I didn't care. The pain from my relationship with this girl had been reduced, if not eliminated. I didn't care about how many drugs I was taking. I cared that my feelings inside went away. They were going away. I preferred to feel nothing rather than anything at all.

However, I was playing with fire. At that time, I was getting a Master of Laws degree from New York University School of Law because, among other things, I ultimately wanted to become a professor. While I was travelling to class one night, I was high on Valium. Before I left for the city, my parents pleaded with me not to drive, because I was "slurring" my words and generally seemed "out of it." Of course, I disregarded them because when you are high on a drug like Valium, you don't feel as messed up as you really are. You just feel happy. I was, though, much more than just happy. As I drove to class I smashed my car right into the back of another vehicle. I was petrified that when they came to the accident scene, the police would know that I was fucked up. Boy, did I get lucky. I convinced the other driver not to call the police because I would pay for the damages in full. I still went to class.

I wasn't lucky the second time. I kept taking massive amounts of Valium because I wanted to escape from the constant uncertainty and lack of control that accompanied my relationship and job. It was all about to catch up with me. To this very day, I remember that morning, as I was walking out of my house, when my mom took me aside and said, "Son, please don't drive, you are in no state to go out ... come back inside." I told her, in my most pleasant way, "Mom, I'm fine, trust me." I was anything but fine. While I was driving to work, Amy called me to say good morning and to have our usual fifteen-minute conversation before work. After about a minute into the call, she started saying, "honey, what is wrong with you! Pull your car over to the side of the road!" I don't even remember hearing her say that, but, according to her, I was babbling incoherently and seemed like I was under the influence of drugs. Well, I was. That was the whole point of walking down the happiness trail.

A few seconds later my conversation with her ended. I passed out behind the wheel of my car. Amazingly, there was a New Jersey State Police car right behind me who saw the whole thing. Apparently, after I passed out behind the wheel, I began to swerve in and out of the four-lane highway. Unfortunately, there was an eighteen-wheeler truck traveling to my right, and I swerved directly into the truck's back tires, which caused me to careen head first into the central divider. I was unconscious, and jammed between my seat and the steering wheel. The officer who approached my car later said, "I didn't know if I would find him alive or dead." I was transported to a local hospital, where I was treated for several injuries, the most important being a head injury that caused bleeding on the frontal lobe of my brain. I was incoherent. I had no idea what was happening around me. I didn't know where I was, who was with me, or why I was there. I was in this semi-conscious state for two days. What I do recall is lying on a table when I arrived and the doctors asking me if I had taken any drugs. I did, in fact, tell them that I had taken a huge amount of Valium. My mom was already there, having heard the news. I guess I vindicated her assumption that I was in no shape to drive.

I came out of it on the third day. My first thought was getting back to Amy. It turns out, as my mom told me, that she had actually visited me in the hospital, even though I had no recollection of that. In any case, my desire to be near her was so strong that I would do anything to get out of the hospital. So, being the lawyer that I was, I invoked my "constitutional right to refuse medical treatment" and left against medical advice. I was still under her control. My health took a backseat to my desire to see her and have sex with her. So, after getting examined by some under-qualified psychiatrists and other medical personnel, I was released from the hospital. The funny thing is, at this point, I didn't give a shit about the uncertainties, instabilities, and impracticalities that characterized my relationship with her. I was in denial. I knew that if I could see her, I could make things better, or she could make me better. The truth was, everything in my life was making me worse and I was diving straight back in, having learned nothing from my near-death experience.

I wasn't just under a delusion or in self-denial. I was actively turning away from the truth about my relationship, my alcohol and drug habit, my disillusionment with the legal profession, and the very issues that had plagued me for years. My accident should have been an eye-opening experience and a call to address the unresolved issues inside of me. Instead, it was nothing more than a small interruption in a whirlwind of an unhealthy life and unhealthy relationship. I had learned nothing from my accident. So the alcohol, drugs, and affair continued. I was willing to do anything even though I could — and almost did — lose everything. As the affair got back to "normal," I would soon discover that alcohol and prescription drugs simply didn't do the job. I needed something more, I wanted more, and I got more — cocaine.

I knew where to get it, although I didn't understand why I suddenly decided that cocaine was something I needed to incorporate into my life. One of my friends from New Jersey, Jason, would be able to get it for me. I have to say, though, that for some time he tried to persuade me not to try coke. He said things like, "man, the way you are, you'll get hooked right away." He was concerned, but I was determined to take the next step towards a new euphoria. I wanted to feel even less pain and more nothingness. I didn't care about feeling happy. I just wanted to feel the absence of depression. If coke could give me a slice of euphoria, that would be great, but I was interested more in what it would take away. On that first night when I did a couple of lines in his apartment, I experienced something new.

That single white line appeared to me like a short road to happiness after a long road of anger and hurt. It would take me to a place that made my problems seem insignificant and unimportant. I sometimes think about people who have near-death experiences, because they frequently say that in those moments, they realize that everything in their life which seemed so difficult, stressful, or overwhelming was really not important. These people often change their lives after such horrible experiences, going on to pursue their passions and never sweating the "small stuff" again. I wanted to feel the same way, but I didn't want to have to endure something like a near-fatal plane crash to get there. When I first did cocaine, I felt liberated from the constraints that I consciously and subconsciously manufactured in my life. I was free, even if it was an odd type of freedom. In this "free" state, I felt like the real me naturally manifested itself. Unfortunately, I found it troubling that cocaine was the catalyst for this most-satisfying state of being.

I remember that night. We were doing coke and for some reason started watching porn videos until about 4:00 a.m. I've never been one to like that kind of stuff, but when I was on drugs, I was simultaneously both my authentic and inauthentic self. I would say everything that was on my mind. I would talk honestly about my life, my relationships, and my feelings. On the other hand, I would do some things that I would never do sober. The porn videos were a good example. Soon, there would be another example. Ultimately, though, what I loved about coke was that you could give up control and just let yourself feel nothing and everything. You don't have to feel the uncomfortable or sad feelings. You don't have to think about uncomfortable thoughts. You don't have to re-live painful memories. You don't have to fight to escape your life. You don't have to run away from yourself. You just feel comfortable in your own skin. Unfortunately, coke couldn't solve a more pressing problem. When I was sober I still wasn't — and couldn't be — me. However, I now had an effective tool to drown out reality even more effectively than alcohol or Valium. Of course, I still used these drugs, but coke was now a part of the group. I felt excited, and, as the title of one of Elizabeth Wuertzel's books says, I wanted "More, Now, Again."

After my first experience with coke, I also had my first "crash." It was horrible. The coke wears off and reality comes crashing down on you. You open your eyes and your problems, almost visible, are staring at your face. The euphoric feelings are gone. Everything seems worse. I was experiencing new emotions that morning, because I had never felt as high as I had been the night before and then as low as I was the next morning. So what did I do? I went to my local gym and exercised on the elliptical machine for about an hour. That was probably stupid, since the coke significantly amps your heart rate and I really didn't need to elevate it again so soon. Anyway, after a few hours, I'd had my first crash, gotten through it, and wanted more coke now, or at least soon.

That's exactly what I got. A few nights later I bought a substantial amount of coke. I was so excited to get smashed again. I was living in the moment. Any conception of the future was drowned out by the difficulties of the past. That night I also purchased a case of Budweiser, took some Valium, and got drunk while having twice as much coke as I'd had on the first occasion. I was so messed up that my nose started bleeding. I didn't care. I was having fun. What really turned me on was that I was finally in control of something. I controlled how much I drank, how much I snorted, when I wanted to stop, and when I wanted to start again. Fuck Amy, Erica, and anyone else. Maybe my habits were destructive, but they were giving me something that I rarely had — control and peace. It didn't matter that these feelings came from a potentially deadly source. Beggars can't be choosers. Drugs were the enemy of the enemy.

I loved doing coke, but eventually I wanted something more — I wanted to have more fun and do the things that would give me as much pleasure as possible. So I started going to a local bar at around 9:00 p.m. and doing coke in the bathroom while I drank. While I genuinely liked being alone, it was also nice to sometimes have conversations with other fucked up people. Then, I would go back home, drink more, do lines, and watch cool movies. I'd do stuff like that and then find a way to tolerate the crash when I went to bed around 6:00 a.m. It became routine.

Unfortunately, though, all this stuff becomes as meaningless as the life from which you are trying to escape. I loved drinking and doing drugs, but I wanted more and more. It's like a new toy that gets old. At that time, I was thinking that there was basically a pyramid of pleasure. Alcohol was at the bottom. Coke was an elevated level of pleasure. Now I wanted to go further up the pyramid. So I tweaked my routine to some extent. When I was doing coke I would go to a strip joint where there were some incredibly hot women. You could also get a lap dance, which was cool.

Then I escalated things again. It's nice to watch girls having sex on TV or teasing you on a couch in a strip joint, but there's nothing more satisfying than the real thing. So one night, while fucked up, I thought about calling an escort service and having sex with a hooker. I'm not sure why I thought of this, other than the fact that I just wanted to have sex. I literally raced towards the yellow pages and looked under the "escort" section. There were so many listings that I didn't know where or how to begin. What did the girls look like? How much did it cost? What things were they willing to do? How long would they stay? After about ten minutes, in a fog of alcohol and coke, I started calling a few places. I started eliminating the ones that were way too expensive, like $500 for an hour, and that narrowed my search somewhat. I was wondering if it also would diminish the beauty of the women that would be available. Each listing had pictures of amazingly beautiful girls and I knew, of course, that the actual girl or girls that came to the apartment would look nothing like this.

Ultimately, I had to choose someplace because I needed to have sex now. So I called several more places, got different quotes, asked about the type of women they had (hair color, age, etc.), and settled on a place not far from my apartment. The deal was that, for $300, she would fuck around with me. I have to say, I was quite nervous. Would I enjoy this? Is this safe? What if she had some disease or something? What if she was ugly so I couldn't get things going? I would be out $300! All of these thoughts rumbled through my head until the door rang. I was on the couch and then slowly walked towards the door. I was so nervous; it was as if the President was walking into the apartment. She represented yet another step down toward the abyss.

Much to my surprise, she was pretty good looking. She had red hair, which I love, and a beautiful body. She was also very nice. In situations like this, you must be on your best behavior because when a hooker comes to your apartment, the driver, usually some brute that could probably kill you with his hands, is waiting outside, watching for any sign of trouble. Anyway, after we exchanged pleasantries, which I thought odd and forced, she said "get comfortable," which meant *take off your clothes*. I initially felt as if I were at the dentist. As much as I wanted this to happen, I also wanted it to end — quickly. I didn't want to feel like some cog in a wheel. The truth is I was still looking for some type of affection and understanding, even though I chose perhaps the least likely place to receive anything other than temporary physical stimulation. It didn't matter to me. Anything that seemed even remotely personal would fill the void for at least a couple of hours.

I didn't feel uncomfortable for very long. The first thing she did was put a condom on me. Then the whole event happened and I enjoyed it. I think she might have enjoyed it too. It was a good experience, but I really don't have much to say about it. I was happy to have good sex. My feelings afterwards were neither happy nor sad. I didn't know how to feel about it, but I was content not to feel anything. The whole thing lasted about 10-15 minutes. Perhaps the most ironic thing is that I didn't feel like I was betraying Amy. For some reason, I didn't care. I think, in the back of my mind, I began to think that she was "having her cake and eating it too." She had the security of a stable marriage while having her emotional needs met on a frequent basis by another man. I was starting to feel used and I didn't like it.

Anyway, when I first had sex with a hooker, it was a bit difficult on both a physical and emotional level. Think about it — you are paying someone to fuck around with you. However, I gained a lot by losing. It was fun, and yet another escape from both the real and fake Adam. It started to happen fairly frequently — weekend after weekend, where I drank beer after beer, snorted coke like it was my last day on earth, and had sex with hooker after hooker. Some of the best times were when I would start partying on a Friday afternoon and go all the way through Sunday — strip clubs, hookers, anything I wanted. See, the thing I liked about the hookers and the strip joints is that, especially with the hookers, I had some type of control over another person. I don't mean that in a bad way, but rather to say that if I paid her it was certain that she would have sex with me. There was no emotional turbulence, people pleasing, or pretense. That made me feel good. I didn't have to be anything. I could just exist and get what I wanted.

Despite all my fucked up habits, which continued throughout the duration of our "relationship," Amy and I kept fooling around, and I kept being the inauthentic people pleaser. Don't get me wrong, the love I gave her was from the real Adam, but the actions were from the people pleaser, whose happiness depended on the stability of our relationship. I eventually became a traitor to my authentic self because, very soon, she betrayed me.

NOTE

1. This is from a press conference Elvis gave on November 20, 1972, before his performance at Madison Square Garden in New York City.

Chapter Eight

The End of the Affair

The Shame and Hurt

Things were about to unravel with Amy. I didn't know it yet, but, based on the red flags, I should have. For nearly four years, I was there for her in every way that I could. She was also there for me. In the end, though, people have to make difficult choices. Right before I was to hear some very hurtful news, things were seemingly getting more stable. Despite my resentment, our conversations started to get deeper and more personal. The sex was more intimate. Of course, I didn't dare mention the drugs and hookers. She had her husband and the drugs and hookers were the equivalent of my "wife."

It was a Friday afternoon when she came to my apartment after a long week at work. I will never forget it. We had sex. When she left, I felt some sense of happiness and fulfillment. At least in some way, I still had her affection. Then the atomic bomb hit. It was a Saturday morning. She called me and asked if I would go for a ride with her to one of the food stores where we lived. Even though I wanted to watch college football on television, I said yes. For some reason, though, as we were going to the store, her driving became erratic. Shit, we almost got into an accident. Clearly, she was flustered and in a very anxious mood. I had never seen her quite like this. It appeared to me that she had something on her mind that she wanted to share with me. Well, she did. About five minutes later, she stopped her car and said, "Honey, I'm pregnant." I stared at her in total amazement. *She's pregnant?* Every time that we'd had sex, I'd used a condom and made sure that it was put on and functioning properly! How could this happen? I wasn't ready to be a father and, quite honestly, I wasn't sure that I wanted children in the first place. So I gave her a measured response, in which I said, "It's ok, relax, everything is going to be ok, I'll be here for you and we'll get through this." Then she said, "It's not your child. I've been trying to have a child with my husband."

Now, this hit me like a bolt of electricity from the electric chair. *You mean you're having an intimate affair with me while, at the same time, trying to get pregnant with him?* If I thought my life was out of control and full of disappointment before, this was definitely superior to anything I'd ever experienced. My first feelings were anger, betrayal, and downright disgust. I wanted to scream, jump out of the car, and never see her again. How could this bitch do this to me? I mean, one day she's on top of me and the next day he's on top of her. How can you rationalize fucking two people at the same time, especially when you are having a child with the one you don't love, but betraying the one you do love? Her explanation — *it's complicated.* It wasn't complicated for me. I felt rejected and thrown away like a piece of trash. I had given my very best to her. I did everything I could to love her, help her, and bring her joy, peace, happiness, and unconditional support. Yet in the end I got fucked — literally and figuratively. All this news did was prove to me that I was less of a true partner to her and more of a means to fill the emotional void in her marriage. When my time was up, when she needed to move on, I was left standing there alone, with no explanation except that "it's complicated." To me, nothing could be simpler.

I never expressed those feelings, though, at least not at that time. This wasn't just about me and her. There was a child involved, a child that would soon bring happiness and joy to her and her family. I felt that, while I could harbor these negative emotions, it would be selfish to express them. Instead of thinking about Amy, I thought about her child. Now that she was pregnant, she needed support, love, and encouragement. Thus, when she needed to see her doctor consistently to assess the status of her pregnancy, assess health issues, and the like, guess who went with her? Me. I took care of her during her pregnancy. I became the rock upon which she could rely. When she feared that there might be something "wrong" with her baby, I reassured her that everything would be fine. I was the support structure that saw her through the pregnancy because her husband was "at work" during all of these doctor visits. I was there for the ups and downs. I reassured her that her second child was going to be beautiful, loveable, and having it was going to be one of the greatest experiences of her life.

I made her smile, while at the same time, inside of me, my authentic self wanted to say, *how could you do this to me! I can't stand you!?* Yet how could I say that? I was looking at ultrasound pictures of a baby inside of her womb and the look in Amy's eyes was of such joy that I had no choice but to share the moment with her. During these moments, I was really not sure if my authentic self was angry at being betrayed, or happy for her that she was so filled with joy. I wasn't sure who I was, but I knew what I needed to do —

support her, and put myself second. In essence, I was doing what I thought I needed to do, instead of what I wanted to do, and that was my biggest mistake.

I never let anyone — especially Amy — know how I was feeling. I was very good at hiding my emotional turmoil and, by all outside appearances, appearing perfectly normal. I was a master of lies and deception. It was very easy for me to convince people that I was "ok" on the outside. However, I could not hide the truth. I could support and love her, but she lied. She betrayed me. She was disloyal. I hated her for it. At the same time, though, I was so happy for her because I knew she'd always wanted a second child. My conflicting emotions were irreconcilable.

After a tremendous amount of introspection, I realized that she was never choosing between me and her husband; instead she was choosing herself and to have the second baby she always wanted. In her eyes, if she stayed with me she would have to end her marriage and probably traumatize her child. If she stayed in the marriage and continued the affair with me, then she may never have had the second child she always wanted. So she made a choice for her and no one else. I never understood that concept until months later. It became a dominant force in my recovery. What I also realized was that, throughout the relationship, I acted with her just like I did with every other person in my life. She was in control. I think she knew that she had the power, and this allowed her to make the choice to be pregnant without telling me. She knew I would be there for her. She knew I would be hurt, yet still stay by her side. I was easy, both emotionally and sexually. She knew she could do what she wanted — and she did. And I stayed until the day she gave birth. I talked to her on the day her baby was born. I was there. Truthfully, I was faking it.

After the birth, we still talked and, every so often, had sex. Every time I saw her, though, I would think of that Saturday morning when she'd told me she was pregnant. I should have told her to fuck off. Instead, I did everything that I didn't want to do and, in so doing, felt everything that I didn't want to feel. Honestly, I was in the situation because of my choices. However, those choices were based on the deeper emotional issues that I'd never resolved. I was afraid to make her angry or upset. I was afraid to feel the shame and guilt. I needed the external approval to mitigate the inner feelings of low self-esteem and insecurity. I needed her to fill the void inside me just like she needed me to fill her emotional void. If I couldn't find external validation, then I couldn't find it anywhere. That is what drove me to make unhealthy choices with Amy, alcohol, drugs, hookers, and the other married woman. When you have no control, when you cannot set boundaries, when your life is based upon the choices and moods of others, then you enter into a spiritual prison. There is no way out. Not through hookers. Not through drugs. Not through anything. Suicide? Yes, that is a way out, but who really wants to do that? I didn't have the desire to die in my late twenties. In the end, Amy stayed in her marriage, and I hope she is happy with her husband who is, truthfully, a great man and father to their two beautiful children. I will always remember the good times, and learn from the bad.

Chapter Nine

The Beginning of Anorexia

I Will Ease Your Mind

In mid-2005, I made a startling discovery. I don't know if I chose it or it chose me. For some reason, my girlfriend's statement from that first time we had sex came back to me:

> *"Adam, you are really heavy, and you need to lose weight."*

When someone told Karen Carpenter that she was a bit "chubby" during the early years of her career, she went on a host of diets and/or food restrictions that ultimately killed her. She died of anorexia at age thirty-two. When Olympic athlete Christy Henrich performed at a national event, one of the judges told her that she was overweight. This sent her into a downward spiral toward anorexia that killed her at the age of thirty-two.

After being disillusioned by the legal profession, by my relationship with Amy, and by the alcohol, drugs, and hookers, I was desperate to have some structure in my life in which things were meaningful and done on my terms. That's when I found a solution in the most unlikely place, at least for me: weight loss. I was 5'8" and 226 pounds. To be clear, though, I did not have anything even remotely resembling an eating disorder at this point. I just felt that it would be a healthy thing to go to the gym, exercise, and watch what I ate. It was something that I did for myself, something that no one else could screw up. I do know, however, that the weight loss idea was not only born out of control issues, but it was also due to the fact that I had terribly low self-esteem and truly hated myself for who I was and what I had done. I honestly felt like an immoral person because I'd had affairs with two married people. I felt like a bad person for abusing alcohol and drugs and for nearly killing myself in that accident. I felt terrible for being such a failure in the legal profession. Ironically, I used to harbor disgust for the "immoral" things that people did and, in a few short years, I became exactly the type of person I'd always despised. I hated myself for it. I had so many questions but no answers. How did my life get to this point? What happened to all of my passions and dreams? Who was this person that I had become? How could I get rid of the moral guilt I felt? The more I thought, the less I could make sense of it all. In fact, I could not deal with these overwhelming feelings. It was simply too much to handle.

Luckily, I found that I could forget about all of these problems by focusing on my weight. I could focus on my body and ignore other people. Nobody can control what you do to your body. People can tell you that you're fat, skinny, ugly, pretty, smart, or stupid. Yet they can't control what you put in your mouth, what you purge from your stomach, what enemas that you use, the laxatives that are always handy, the water pills that keep you from feeling bloated, and, of course, the excessive exercise that compensates for any episodes of binge eating. Excessive exercise is particularly gratifying; you cannot believe how much your body can handle until you push it to its maximum limits. The crazy thing is, it's so difficult to know where your body's limits are. Thus, my *de facto* limit when I was anorexic was, *my body has had enough when I am about to faint*. Not a bad calibration. Also, if the exercise wasn't enough, I had tools at my disposal: water pills, laxatives, vomiting, and anything else to make me look thin. If I could be in control of my weight, I could be in control of other people. If I could control other people, I could control my feelings. I had found the Holy Grail.

My fixation now became on losing weight. After about one month, my weight went from 226 pounds to 206 pounds. I was so proud of myself. I lost twenty pounds through commitment, will power, and a desire to change my health and appearance. I was finally becoming addicted to a good thing. I kept telling myself how dieting was wonderful because it improves "good" cholesterol and reduces "bad" cholesterol levels, works wonders for your mood, your cardiovascular system, and brain function. So when I started dieting after the coke (which I'd quit after my last horrific crash), the job firings, the hookers, the strip clubs, and the porn, I felt like I was back on the right track. I had finally found a way to control my life! It was through my weight — that was the answer. I didn't realize that for so many years I had been searching for happiness in everything external to me, when the one thing that put a smile on my face was internal and universal — me. This was something that I couldn't fuck up, right?

Shortly thereafter, I signed a three-year contract with Bally's Health Club so that I could work out at their gym every day. As it turns out, this was a rip-off, because rarely do people work out at the same gym for three years. You often get tired of going to the same place, doing the same exercise, and seeing the same steroid-filled muscle-freaks whose dicks are likely to fall off because of the rampant drug use. Just the smell of the place is nauseating. Whatever the case, I stopped going after about two years, but nonetheless had to pay for the remaining year. It really was no big deal, though, because during those first two years I made remarkable strides. I was intent on picking out the machine that would burn the most calories as quickly as possible and the elliptical machine was a perfect fit. Then, however, I found something better: spinning class. What a rush. Basically, in the spinning room, you ride on a stationary bike for about fifty minutes while inspirational music is blaring and, at certain intervals, you adjust the resistance on the bike to make it more difficult. It was a grueling workout, but at the end it felt great. I was burning massive amounts of calories. Slowly, but surely, my mind was shifting. I was beginning to focus on exercise not for the purpose of increasing health, but for decreasing weight. I kept repeating that mantra in my head:

> *"Adam, you are really heavy, and you need to lose weight."*

This statement, of course, wasn't the ultimate cause of what was to come. My girl did not single-handedly fuck up my relationship with food and weight. If that were true, then any dipshit who gets his or her heart broken would venture into the world of anorexia or bulimia. It was, instead, the culmination of a life filled with rejection, disappointment, and disillusionment. I wasn't anywhere near that, though. I just kept spinning, even though I would soon begin spinning out of control.

My 20-pound weight loss brought me a sense of happiness and accomplishment. I loved watching my body get thinner. It empowered me. It motivated me to lose more weight, exercise harder, and restrict my food intake. However, I love food, so that was an obstacle. I needed a plan. Remember all of those Valium pills that my doctor gave me? I didn't have that many left, so I paid him a visit and again pretended to have a debilitating anxiety problem (I'm a good actor) and, once again, I got more Valium than I could handle. I began to create a structured plan. I would go to the gym around 7:00 p.m. each night and, over the course of an hour, burn about 800 calories on the elliptical machine, and then go to a store where they served healthy "smoothies." I would purchase the diet peach smoothie, which had all the ingredients that were supposed to help you lose weight. It was only about 300 calories, so I knew I would still be hungry after I drank it. However, that was addressed by the second part of my plan — the Valium.

So, after drinking the smoothie, I would turn on the TV and take 20mg of Valium, which knocked me out in about forty-five minutes. Therefore, I was physically unable to consume more food because I was unconscious. The only problem with this, of course, is that every morning I woke up with urine all over myself because my central nervous system was so depressed that I could not actually wake up and control my bodily functions. To me, it was a small price to pay for losing weight. My makeshift method was successful, as it brought me down to 186 pounds, 18 pounds lighter than when I had started the Valium. A few of my friends noticed the difference, and mentioned how good I looked. Good? Are you fucking kidding me? I was still obese! My face was pale because of all the Valium I was taking. I had a long, long way to go. Although, for the first time in a long time, I was receiving genuine compliments for something that I had done on my own terms and through my own effort. That was so wonderful, empowering, and motivating.

Anorexia was not even in my lexicon at this point. To me, anorexics were skeletal young girls who would do anything to look like the next beautiful girl on *Vogue Magazine*. Being 5'8" and 186 pounds surely left more room for weight loss and there was not a single person in the universe who would say that additional weight loss was not healthy. That, however, isn't my point. You don't need to be anorexic to feel the immense euphoria when the scale nudges down just a bit further. Why? You become the master of your universe — the control freak — the essential cure for all of the problems of shame, guilt, self-hatred, and low self-esteem that we anorexics carry like a scarlet letter. What I would find out, however, is that anorexia doesn't give you control; it actually takes it away.

Chapter Ten

Anorexia and the New Doctor

The Joy Is Over

It was late 2005. My affair was, for all purposes, over. Once in a while we saw each other, but my heart was no longer in it. I felt like I'd had enough of the emotional turmoil. It was one of the hardest things I've ever done, but I just had to distance myself physically and emotionally. The relationship had become unhealthy and the writing was on the wall. Heck, the writing had been on the wall for a long time, but I was somehow illiterate. I had no job. What was I going to do? I had no idea. Except for one thing — I was going to lose more weight.

As 2006 approached, I was 186 pounds, still fucking around on the ellipti-cal at Bally's and, as always, annoyed by those loud screams of the muscle freaks who thought that lifting 350 pounds somehow guaranteed them a spot in heaven. While weight loss was on my mind, it hadn't yet taken such a crippling hold on me. As I looked at my life, I tried to convince myself that things would get better. *I will eventually be in a healthy relationship and life will get back to normal. I'm just going through a bad time.* That line from *American Beauty*, "never underestimate the power of denial," was vindicated by my actions.

I was dead wrong. Things weren't going to get better. Those positive thoughts at that time were the best moments that I would have for the next five years. My weight slowly but surely crept downward. A week later I weighed 180 pounds. Let's put this in perspective. For someone who is 5'8," the recommended weight range is 145-157 pounds. So I was twenty-three pounds away from the outermost limit of that range. My celebration, though, wasn't tainted in any way. I had lost forty-six pounds through hard work, determination, and a sheer will to look good. People noticed. I got compliments from friends and anyone else who had seen me when I was forty-six pounds heavier. I do recall that one night, when I came home, my mom took me into the living room and said, "son, you look wonderful, I am so proud of you, but don't lose any more weight, you look good the way you are." She was an Italian mother, so husky people are considered "normal."

Remember that I said that anorexia didn't yet have a crippling hold on me? Well, my mother's statement tightened its grasp. My poor mom, she said the wrong thing in the wrong place at the wrong time. All of a sudden, my mom is asking me *not* to do something? She is pleading with me not to lose any more weight? This was too good to be true. Instead of being controlled, I finally had control over another person in my life. The power dynamic had flipped. My mom was concerned about me and the only way she could get her way was through my consent. No more bullshit or lies from my girlfriend, friends, lawyers, or anyone else. This was the beginning of a long road of revenge — revenge through the very control that I felt was exercised over me for so long. This was my time to strike back at the world.

Even though I was about to graduate with my Master of Laws degree from NYU, it meant nothing to me. I had no passions anymore. I had no desires to be, or to become something. I just was. I was a walking corpse. I didn't believe in anything. I didn't stand for anything. I didn't hope for anything. I wasn't passionate about what could be, what might be, or what could be created. I just was.

My response to my mom's comment, and my state of mind, was to destroy my body further and lose more weight. I went to the liquor store and purchased beer, a pack of cigarettes, and then I called Jason. I hoped that he would answer the phone and have some coke to sell me. My dream came true. He answered, and he knew immediately why I called. He said, in a humorous way, "you son of a bitch, I'd knew you'd come back." He told me that he could get some from one of his friends. I told him that I had two hundred dollars on me and to get a lot of it. I was so excited. I could escape from reality again and immerse myself in a world of euphoria and effervescence. I had such a wonderful night in my apartment, at least by my standards — beer, porn, coke, hookers, and then I ate the best pizza in town.

Since I had so much of the shit and was having such a good time, I decided to keep partying through the weekend. So Friday turned into Saturday and I went to my local strip club, got myself a few lap dances, and asked one of the strippers if she wanted to come back to my apartment and "party" with me. Well, I wasn't that lucky. Gratefully, or sadly, not all was lost. When I drove back to my apartment, out of sheer luck, there was a hooker leaving someone else's apartment building. In my drug and alcohol infected mind, I thought, *well, I didn't "order" her, but what do I have to lose by asking her to stick around?* I thought she, along with whoever was in the car about to pick her up, would tell me to fuck off. Notwithstanding, I decided to ask, thinking that "there is no such thing as a stupid question." Well, she agreed to hook up with me and came back to the apartment. It was fun — and expensive. I enjoyed the temporary happiness, even though my life was a joke.

I knew, though, that the crash would eventually come, and it did like a tsunami. On Sunday, after that awful coke-fueled binge weekend, I felt so unbelievably horrible, both on an emotional and physical level. I was tired, depressed, angry, and sad. I knew I needed help. However, I didn't necessarily want help. Part of me wanted to continue on the path to self-destruction, if only because it provided me with the certainty of physical and psychological pleasure. For me, "recovery" or getting "help" meant giving up all of these habits and becoming a "new" person, which was very scary due to the issues I would have to confront and the habits I would have to abandon. Despite these emotions, my rational mind prevailed. I made what I thought was an informed decision to see a psychiatrist and therapist. I was destroying my body with drugs and alcohol. I needed help on so many issues, from what was currently going on in my life to the horrible, deep feelings of depression and inadequacy that had plagued me from a very young age.

Furthermore, those existential questions that I frequently asked, such as, *why are we here? What is the purpose of life? Why do I feel so unhappy that it feels so painful?* still affected me. I was struggling with issues and questions that I had neither the intellect nor the knowledge to answer. So a psychiatrist and therapist seemed like a logical, if not desperate, solution. Yet I needed more than logic to solve these problems. When you feel miserable, but cannot point to any reason, you get scared. It makes you feel that you're living with a condition that has no cause and has no end. If that's true, I thought, my attempt to seek help would be futile. I just didn't know. I had to try, though, because if I didn't make the attempt now, maybe I wouldn't in the future. Maybe suicide was the only cure.

The first session was with a psychiatrist, Dr. Metcalf, who was warm, welcoming, and who put me at ease. After going through a standard questionnaire in which she familiarized herself with my background, we began to discuss my feelings, the symptoms I was experiencing, and all of the things that a psychiatrist discusses with a patient. She diagnosed me with major depressive disorder and prescribed the drugs Lamictal and Paxil. I was a bit taken aback by the prescription of two drugs after one session but, given the emotional pain that I was experiencing, I decided to take these drugs as prescribed. Unfortunately, however, they really did not help me, which is not uncommon. It often takes several attempts to find the right medications that will effectively treat the symptoms affecting a particular person. For me, at that moment, I cared less about the treatment efficacy than I did about the fact that I was finally trying to get help on truthful terms. I was going to confront the issues that had resulted from my feelings of worthlessness, low self-esteem, and self-hate. Don't get me wrong — there were many days when I wanted to walk out and go right back to a coke and alcohol-fueled binge. I was doing my best, however, to run towards instead of away from my life.

I soon began to see my therapist, Dr. Fratello. She was a very nice woman, very experienced in dealing with patients with major depressive disorder and other mental illnesses. She also had an uncanny ability to relate to her patients in a personal, warm, and sensitive way, and that made for a very comfortable experience. I felt that I could be open, honest, and forthright about my innermost thoughts and feelings. We decided to see each other on a weekly basis and, for the first several weeks, things went very well. We used a form of treatment called cognitive behavioral therapy, in which I examined the behavioral patterns that allowed me to understand why I engaged in certain actions during various aspects of my life, namely the affairs, the alcohol, drugs, and hookers.

It was really a cathartic process because it took the "blame" away from my past actions. I was taught not to feel bad or immoral about my prior choices. Cognitive behavioral therapy helped me understand why I was using cocaine at a particular point in my life and why I was fucking hookers. It was because I was in such serious pain and seeking validation in any form possible that would allow the pain to subside. I was seeking love and affection. This type of therapy was a soothing process because it allowed me to feel like the mistakes I'd made were not universally "my fault." Instead, they were a type of defense mechanism designed to take away the negativity and bring some peace into my life. The therapy helped me make sense of what appeared to be a senseless experience. I still hated myself, though, and that was the real hurdle to overcome, because self-hatred is one of anorexia's best friends.

Then something happened in one of our sessions that I could not believe and you will probably not believe. I was discussing the idea of suicide and how I sometimes thought that it might be a rational way of ending the ongoing emotional pain that people feel in their lives. Think about it — mental illness, whether it is depression, bi-polar disorder, or schizophrenia, can last a lifetime and can cause unending despair. So I was asking my therapist if she ever thought suicide could be a "rational" decision; specifically, could it be the right decision to end one's life for the purpose of escaping the horrible pain of mental anguish? People refuse medical treatment in the latter stages of terminal illnesses because they no longer want to suffer the pain and indignity of the dying process. Why should mental anguish be any different?

My therapist, of course, tried to provide me with the "don't give up" explanation, which I immediately found repulsive. I hate platitudes — general statements that are meant to apply to everyone. They have nothing to do with individualized treatment. They don't reflect attention to, or specific concerns about the individual. Don't give up? Fuck you. Tell that to a terminally ill cancer patient. Don't give up? Fuck you. That wasn't the worst part. What happened next, well, I wouldn't say it shocked me. That would be an understatement. It simply created an emotional feeling that I never experienced before. Have you ever had that happen? When something happens that you've never experienced before, you can sometimes have an emotional reaction that you cannot categorize into any of the emotional compartments that you've recalled from past experience. It's a cross between feeling like a child, yet feeling so old that you don't remember what it used to be like to feel anything.

Here's what happened. Dr. Fratello was beginning to tell me why suicide is never an option because, unlike terminally ill cancer patients, people with mental illnesses do get better over time. I thought that was bullshit. As she said this, she pulled her chair over to me, placed her hand on my leg, and smiled at me. After about five seconds, she moved away from me. What should I have done? Maybe I should have pulled my chair back. Maybe I should have put her hand off my thigh. Then I stopped. I was not going to blame myself for what she did. The truth was that I was scared, but not in the traditional way. I didn't fear harm. I feared the unfamiliarity of the situation. I was in unchartered waters. I didn't know what she was doing. So I did something maybe I shouldn't have done. I made an assumption that she was harmless and just acting in a sensitive and warm manner.

However, I left the meeting feeling violated. Despite my assumption, I had this feeling that there was something more going on there. It didn't make sense to me, though, because it seemed so crazy. In fact, the idea was so bizarre that it was easy for me to just dismiss it as absurd. Also, I was a pretty fucked up person, so I was not entirely confident in my assessment. However, I couldn't shake my gut feeling. I'm not a stupid or naïve person. *Maybe she did make a pass at me.* That would be such a violation of any and every professional rule of ethics that she would lose not only her license but could also face prosecution. I kept going over and over it in my head. People would think I was crazy if I brought this up. After all, on the surface, the act itself would seem harmless. The only thing she did was touch my thigh. Yet that really wasn't normal in the therapist-patient relationship, was it? How many therapists touched their patients like that? Was I getting any help here? Was I getting therapy for my problems? Maybe I was the therapist and she was the patient. I knew what I had to do. I had to go back and see how this shit was going to play out.

So I went to the next session scared, nervous, and uncertain. In addition to all of my emotions, I was still hoping, perhaps with futility, that Dr. Fratello would actually be able to help me through my emotional turmoil. I sat in the waiting room and looked at a poster that had a list of ten "inspirational" quotes for us desperate souls. Guess what the last one was? "Don't give up." How about, "Give me a fucking break." Anyway, when she called me into her office, I was tense but acted as normally as possible. After all, what the fuck was I supposed to do? Sit there and act like I was about to be molested?

So we sat there and, as usually happened in therapy, we started with the typical small talk. *How are you doing? How was your day?* Questions that are incapable of eliciting any meaningful answers, unless, of course, something overwhelmingly positive or negative has happened. Even then, those answers would be rather banal because extreme emotion, in any direction, is the backbone of people dealing with mental illnesses. Soon we resumed our discussion of suicide, which was more of a debate than a therapeutic exercise. It was as if I was no longer getting any help for my issues, but instead engaging in a lively debate with a friend. So I tried to steer the conversation back to how I was feeling, what I was experiencing, and what I needed to do to get better. All of her "answers" or "suggestions" were the same as what I had heard from other therapists or any self-help book that could be found in Barnes and Noble. In other words, they threatened to make me worse, not better. We never talked about any of my intimate, personal experiences with the kind of depth that I needed. In other words, I needed an original perspective — from a professional — to help me understand my actions and get through this difficult time in my life. Yet, I felt like the touch on my thigh broke something and nearly eliminated that possibility. I just didn't feel right about our relationship. Trusting her with more personal information would be difficult for me, because I wasn't sure if she could help me anymore.

My uncertainties regarding her motivations soon became quite clear. In our next session, Dr. Fratello said something that made me curious, if not for any other reason, for its originality. She told me that, in her opinion, traditional cognitive behavioral therapy might not be the most effective way to treat the various issues with which I was struggling. She said it in a professional way, as if it were based on an empirical diagnosis. I was, of course, skeptical at first, because I had never known any other methods of therapeutic analysis. Yet I was intrigued. I'm the type of person who never likes to shut out opportunities, especially ones that I've never experienced. That's the whole point of life, isn't it?

So I inquired further. In a serious and somewhat disengaged tone, Dr. Fratello said that she operated a substantial part of her practice from home, where she had an office and engaged in alternative types of therapy. I should have seen the red flags pop up then. I asked her, what kind of alternative therapy? She said things like meditation, muscle relaxation, deep breathing, positive affirmations, and other "alternative" but not totally unfathomable or untried methods. She informed me that if I ever wanted to explore this avenue, I would be welcome to do so. I appreciated that statement, because it didn't feel like I was being lulled or coerced into some type of scheme, but rather given a different opportunity to heal myself. Maybe the touch on the thigh was innocuous after all. Even if it was not, maybe I was misinterpreting the feelings and intentions behind the touch. It's hard to say, because with the alcohol, Valium, and coke going through my system regularly, I was ready to jump at anything that might help me. Logic and reason took a back seat to hope.

I wasn't ready to jump into "alternative" therapy just yet. Fuck, I could just go on the internet to see what all the shit was about. However, as our sessions became more normalized, i.e., she didn't touch me, I agreed to go see her at her home and try some new therapeutic techniques. After all, while I was feeling a bit better, I continued to feel like my life, and all the actions that supported it, was based on a foundation without meaning. During this time, though, there was a silver lining. My weight had dropped from 186 to 178 pounds. The elliptical machine and spinning classes were doing a fine job of giving me some purpose. Unfortunately, at this point, the weight loss could not be my "everything," as I was still anchored by hate, depression, and isolation.

So I went to Dr. Fratello's house, which was modest but well-kept. She answered the door smiling and quickly ushered me into her office, which was very professional in its appearance. We started talking like we did during our normal sessions and then proceeded into the types of meditative exercises that she had described in our earlier sessions. I would just sit there, close my eyes, and listen to the sound of my breath. It felt strange and scary, almost as if my mind was creating a combination of the most depraved and happy thoughts at the same time. The silence created a tidal wave of thoughts that made me hate the very idea of feeling. I wanted to stop and start screaming. I estimate that I was only able to do it for about one minute before I spoke and said, "Wow, this is weird," to which she replied, "It takes practice." I was thinking to myself, *what takes practice, sitting here like a dope in silence and listening to my breath and heartbeat? Hey, maybe this works for some people, but not me!* Of course, I reluctantly agreed to try again in future sessions. Remember, I'm a "people pleaser" — I don't say no — I say yes.

Then she mentioned that other thing — muscle relaxation, and I was thinking, *how the fuck do you achieve muscle relaxation through a mental exercise?* More importantly, I still didn't feel that I was getting effective — or attentive — treatment for issues that had driven me to treatment. I didn't know how all these techniques would help me. Instead, I wanted to talk about my problems. I wanted to talk about what had happened with my Amy. I wanted to talk about how jaded I was by the legal profession. I wanted to talk about how my life, my feelings, my well-being, and my choices, were all out of control. I wanted to talk about the alcohol, drugs, and hookers. We didn't talk about any of that. In essence, we never talked about me.

Anyway, it was on to muscle relaxation. We went into Dr. Fratello's relaxation room. There were dimmed lights everywhere, a leather table, a soothing atmosphere, and the general sense that the "real" world was simply not welcome in this place. Of course, she didn't explain what she was going to do or, for that matter, what I was going to do. However, the Adam who had no voice, who was filled with shame and self-hatred, could not possibly come up with any reason or excuse to refuse these "alternate" therapeutic modalities. Truthfully, I was thinking that I should leave the room immediately. For some reason, though, I couldn't. I was afraid of making her angry. I was afraid of hurting her feelings. I was a man but still a child.

So the first thing she did with respect to this "muscle relaxation" exercise was to speak professionally and openly. She was trying to put me at ease, which was successful. I was vulnerable, and she was probably aware of that. She then asked me to take off my shirt and lie down on the leather table. I immediately thought that things were now outside the box, although she kept telling me that the purpose was to relieve tension throughout my body and mind. She obviously was going to give me a massage. After about two minutes, I became uncomfortable with the way she was touching me. I felt like I was being violated. To say the least, it allowed me to realize that the touch on the thigh in her office was not innocent at all. Likewise, this "muscle relaxation" exercise, to the extent that it had any therapeutic benefit, was for her, not me.

So, did I speak up? No. Why? Why didn't I end this "session" when I felt this way? I was afraid. I thought she would get furious at me and start denying everything. I thought I would feel embarrassed and humiliated. Even though I knew with certainty that I was being violated, I still doubted myself. I just wanted the entire situation to be calm and peaceful, and I didn't want her to feel bad or hurt. So I let myself get hurt because I perceived that the hurt I would feel for asserting myself would be greater than the hurt I felt from just lying there, being touched inappropriately. Essentially, I didn't have the ability to stand up for myself and draw the types of boundaries that would have protected my physical and emotional well-being. It was precisely these feelings, and this situation, that fueled my self-hatred. I was so angry for letting her, and other people, treat me like shit. I blamed myself for all the times when I was exploited and just sat there in silence. Truthfully, my inability to protect myself resulted from the fact that I didn't think I was worthy enough to assert myself and tell her to stop. I had no self-esteem. I wasn't a victim of Dr. Fratello. I was a victim of me.

Soon thereafter I stopped the sessions. I also stopped the medications because they weren't helping me. It would be only after I moved to my new city that I found the right medications and treatment to make a true recovery. The true injury that I suffered there came in part from the realization, however irrational, that any treatment I sought for depression and all of the other issues I've talked about might be hopeless. It was at this point that my feelings regarding mental illnesses and terminal illnesses merged. I started to see very few differences between the two. My pain was real and palpable. The idea, though, that it could be permanent, was the nail in the coffin. That's why suicide so involuntarily came to my mind. It was the equivalent to removing life-sustaining medical care for the cancer-stricken patient. Every day I lived, I was breathing life into an artificial existence with no spiritual or emotional capacity to realize my creative potentials. While I was able to get away from this situation, I couldn't get away from myself. I put my power and control in her rather than myself. I was, essentially, the enemy of myself.

Then I shut the door and went back to the "darker" side of my reality. For me, though, the darker side was my version of happiness. In yet another ten days, I was down to 173 pounds. My mood suddenly shifted. Instead of being proud of my weight loss, I became ecstatic. I now "owned" something that made me feel good about myself. I created happiness on my own terms, and it was based upon the number on a scale. My weight loss efforts soon began to occupy a more central role in my life. Of course, based on the relevant height/weight charts, I knew I was still overweight because I was not between 145-157 pounds. Yet I was inching closer, and that felt good, at least for the moment. I was gaining control over my body. I kept gaining by losing. Every ounce meant, to me, a step toward liberation. I felt like I was the "underdog" and that my weight and body image would be the force to help me become a better me.

The promise that I felt from starvation and weight loss necessitated a change in my routine. For the next ten days, I exercised with much more intensity, often twice a day. I ate as little as possible and could literally feel the weight melting off of me. I loved standing in front of the mirror and grabbing the loose skin that used to be filled with fat. When I stepped on the scale again, it was pure rapture: 166 pounds. Still eleven pounds over the limit for individuals of my height, but still sixty pounds less than that fat slob who took up too much of the world's space. At least for now, I had some sense of purpose. I could find solace in the fact that I could accomplish something.

My life outside of this little world, however, was out of control. When I say that things were *going* out of control, I mean that things *were* out of control. I wasn't simply asking existential questions like: *Why are we here? What's the purpose in life? What am I meant to do?* To me, those questions had become immature and silly. I no longer had to ask because I already knew. There was nothing to live for because life itself was nothingness and meaninglessness. It was a gigantic void of space where people made up stories about "love," Santa Claus, the tooth fairy, the Easter Bunny, organized religion, and whatever else helped us to make sense of our senseless existence. To me, it all seemed like bullshit. Love wasn't something, or anything, because it wasn't permanent. Relationships always fall apart after a certain time. Marriages end in divorce. Even those relationships that lasted seemed to transform into more of a friendship. Santa Claus, being as fat as he was depicted, simply could not have travelled all over the world in twenty-four hours with gifts that probably weighed close to one-hundred thousand tons, with reindeer that could never support such a burden. Ok, so that's gone. Now, the tooth fairy warrants no further explanation.

As far as the Easter Bunny, well, it took me about seventy seconds to realize that some big white bunny doesn't hop around the country holding two-hundred and fifty million Easter baskets. I was a waiter once and couldn't even balance three plates in my hands. Then we have organized religion that, every Sunday, or whatever day you choose to go to church, makes you feel like shit for everything you did or did not do. It also makes the world seem like a miserable place and emphasizes that we must sacrifice ourselves and deny ourselves earthly pleasures in order to enter the Kingdom. Oh, and during lent, we can't eat meat on Fridays. Now, do you think God, when deciding who to bring into his Kingdom, gives a fuck about whether you had a steak on a Friday afternoon during lent in 1968? No. During these times, my anger was often replaced by hurt. I was sad because, as a child and young adult, the world was presented to me in a way that was completely false. Now that I knew the truth, I was confused. I was also upset. I didn't know how to find meaning for myself.

I tried desperately to suppress these feelings through alcohol and drug use. I still had some coke/hooker parties, but it just wasn't the same anymore. You know when you try to go back and re-live some of the best memories of your life? For some reason, they just aren't the same. I think it's because we change. Our feelings change, our perspective changes, and our emotional state changes. Meaningless pleasures can no longer serve as the band-aid for the pain that we feel when nothingness pays a visit to our life and makes its permanent residence in our hearts. I remember that night. I was drinking a lot of beer, but I couldn't get drunk. I was snorting a lot of coke, but it didn't have the same effect and, whatever effect it did have, it made me feel more depressed than ever. And when my hooker came, it wasn't a pleasurable experience. I felt very scared on that night. I hated my reality with a passion, and my coping mechanisms — the drugs, the alcohol, and the hookers — weren't taking the pain away anymore. So I was stuck with reality one hundred percent of the time. I needed more of something. So I did something I had never done. I wrote a poem. Now, I am no poet, so the poem sucked, but it did convey my misery at the time:

"Blackened"
I cry in reverse, my tears drying up my drowning soul
Darkness remains my only friend,
The last day upon which this misery will end
You think the world is above you,
But it is nothing more than believing that the sunlight is your own
Nothing more than a grand design to control our becoming
And arrest my destiny
I have nothing but blackness;
I am nothing but emptiness
Let my demons marry me
For my last days are but the truest beginning
This is my day
It is so brightly black and so terribly warm.
This is my life

I also did something else — for myself and own well-being. Since my passion was to someday become a law professor, I decided to send my resume to every law school that was hiring and looking for candidates for the fall of 2007. Well, I got so many rejection letters that I felt academically raped (I say this in a half-joking way). However, I did get one interview. At that time, the professors responsible for conducting the interview were in Washington, D.C., so I travelled there and met them for approximately thirty minutes. I really enjoyed our conversation and, more importantly, they seemed like great people. After the interview, as I was driving back to New Jersey, I tried not to get my hopes up, but I did think I had a chance to get the job. It's funny, but hope, while sometimes dangerous, can be cathartic when your life is out of control.

Regardless, I knew, deep down, that no matter what happened with the job, I would ultimately have to deal with the emotional issues that were so strongly affecting my life. I would have to admit to the hurt and betrayal that I'd experienced. I would have to cry and admit that my anger was just a mask for the pain that I felt inside. I didn't have the courage to do that yet. I didn't want to talk about the affairs, the alcohol, the drugs, the hookers, or the legal profession. I still needed to escape.

Even if the drugs and alcohol didn't help me on that night, I still had my exercise regimen. I still had weight loss. The next time I went to Bally's, the elliptical was right there waiting for me. Just as I was about to begin my workout, which was really a daily torture session, I noticed a case filled with energy drinks, from Red Bull to other shit that I never heard of. I immediately looked past the Red Bull into the more unknown but cool-looking stuff. I asked one of the trainers, what exactly does the stuff do? He said, "It increases your body's metabolism during the workout so that you burn more calories." I had struck gold. I bought two of the bottles and raced towards the elliptical.

It was an amazing, therapeutic experience. I had never exercised with such intensity in my life. My heart rate peaked at 172 beats per minute. I felt euphoric. I felt important. I felt like I was accomplishing something that very few people could. Most importantly, I felt in control. I had an outlet where I was the boss. No one could touch me. No one could criticize me. My shame was replaced by feeling accomplished. My self-esteem suddenly made me feel worthy of loving and being loved. And I did this myself. I was beginning to create a new secret world that filled my emotional void, a void that coke, hookers, and alcohol could no longer fill. Then I went on the scale: 159 pounds. I'd lost another seven pounds. So far, I had lost sixty-eight pounds, and the shame, self-hatred, guilt, and low self-esteem was all subsiding, at least for a few hours. It always came back, but the peace I felt during those few hours made me want to stay on that elliptical until I couldn't stand it anymore.

Chapter Eleven

Exercise

I Can't Help But Love You

I never did coke again. I never fucked a hooker again. I never gave much more than a half-hearted effort at anything I did except for my exercise. There was no point. It was an endless cycle of joy and misery. I had no respect for anyone or anything, including myself. Yet my weight and body image were starting to provide me with a life of respect and control. I still didn't know that I was on the path towards anorexia. I thought I was on the path towards the type of free and authentic experience that I had always envisioned.

As the end of 2006 came around, I was working out furiously on the elliptical machine. Once in a while, I would talk to Amy. At that point, our relationship was not strained or tense. Time had passed. I had somehow gotten over the hurt feelings, and had come to terms with the notions of betrayal and desire to cut her out of my life. We talked about her new child, family, job, and all those other common things that people discuss. We became friends, and are to this day; after several turbulent years while I was struggling with anorexia, we have managed to get back in touch. Sometimes when there are happy endings, even when they are in the wake of awful experiences, you see the power of the human soul to forgive and move forward to create new realities and possibilities.

It was at this time that I happily discovered a new source of pleasure. You have to understand that I was always on the look-out for new and interesting ways of making myself happy. Well, there was this new "massage" parlor that had been built about ten minutes from my house, and the advertisement showed Korean women in seductive poses. I thought, *shit, maybe these cute girls will give me a happy ending!* At least it was worth a shot. So I went to the massage place and they had only one dressing room — for the men. Some guy said, "Take everything off and put this towel around you." After that, we were escorted into a beautiful room with nice candles, bamboo, and a beautiful scent. Then my massage therapist came in and gave me a wonderful massage. I almost fell asleep. After about forty-five minutes, she started massaging my arms, my hands, and my legs. In about two minutes, my questions and curiosities were answered. This place became a fixture for some time.

The holidays were nearing and I didn't give a shit. I didn't want to see or talk to people. I didn't want to receive gifts. There was nothing to celebrate except my low fucking self-esteem. Indeed, as much as I enjoyed the earthly pleasures in which I was indulging, there was part of me that felt like a scumbag for doing these things. I just didn't have a good relationship with myself. I was still hoping, though, that I might get the teaching position, because the opportunity to shape people's lives, values, and to inspire them is something that means a lot to me.

Fortunately, or perhaps unfortunately, because all of my other coping mechanisms were slowly failing, I kept increasing the duration and intensity of my workouts. At this point, I didn't have many friends because I had begun to isolate myself from the world. I had become consumed with my own thoughts and existence. I wanted to know why I was in this fucked up situation. I wanted to know how I had so grossly veered off my path. These unanswerable questions kept attacking my mind even though I no longer knew what my destiny was, or what I was meant to do in this world. I didn't want to go out with people, socialize, or do anything but think about my pain. Why couldn't I talk to anybody? Nobody would understand. Nobody would be able to help me. They would give me cookie-cutter advice. So I didn't want to waste my time trying to get help in all the wrong places. I'd been there and, as you now know, done that. Also, as wonderful as they are, my parents truly didn't understand the depths of my despair because I never voiced the severity of my pain.

The exercise served so many functions. It blinded me to myself. It submerged me in a world of denial and avoidance. The logical answer, therefore, was to increase the intensity. When I went to Bally's, I stayed on the elliptical machine for ninety minutes and burned approximately 1,500 calories, which was my highest number yet. I was delighted by this achievement and, for a short period of time, I felt happiness instead of despair, purpose instead of meaninglessness, and authenticity instead of fakeness. I felt accomplished, empowered, and elite: nobody could do what I just did. Then I thought of Lance Armstrong. Oh well. More importantly, though, nobody could make me stop doing what I was doing. Of course, it didn't erase the feelings that were festering inside of me. What it did do, however, was suppress them. If I could focus on my exercise and weight, then I wouldn't have to focus on my issues, and they wouldn't have to focus on me.

At this point, I was slowly becoming addicted to weight loss. While I cherished my daily exercise routine, it was starting to become a bit less important than that number I saw on the scale. As my world — and body — began to shrink, I became more and more obsessed with that number. I don't know if I realized it then, but the scale was replacing the role of my parents, my colleagues, Amy, and everyone else; it was becoming the only arbiter of my self-esteem. It was the judge and jury, truth vs. falsity, victory over defeat. I needed the scale to show me that I was losing weight, just like I needed the approval of everyone around me. That number was becoming my boss and my world.

You can imagine, therefore, the trepidation as I stepped on the scale later that week. The scale ceased to be an object. It was a person, and every time I walked towards it I prayed for that affirmation that even drugs and prostitutes could not give me. Well, the scale read 153 pounds. Another 6-pound weight loss and a total weight loss of seventy-three pounds. This only motivated me to exercise more: not 5-6 times a week as I had been doing, but 9-12 times a week, which often meant twice in one day. At this point, I no longer had a weight loss goal. I just wanted to keep losing and losing because that meant I was gaining and gaining. Ironically, I could use the scale to defend my behavior. If anyone ever mentioned anything about my weight, I could simply respond that it was in the "normal' range. For the first time in my life, I was making positive changes on my own. I was, however, under a dangerous delusion. While I finally thought that I was walking away from a world where I had always felt controlled, taken advantage of, and abused, I didn't realize that I was walking right back into one.

I really wanted to go somewhere but I was nowhere. I was slowly beginning a transformative process that would ultimately take control of my life and my health. In early 2007, however, it sure didn't seem like that. Things just seemed as they always had. Yes, the exercise and weight loss was making me happy and giving me a source of control. Yet, no matter what I tried, I could not erase the sheer, penetrating feelings of hopelessness and disillusionment that woke me up in the morning and wouldn't let me go to sleep at night. The constant emotional pain, self-hatred, and powerlessness I tried so desperately to erase through drugs, alcohol, affairs, hookers, and anything else wouldn't go away. I thought that maybe there was no hope for me. I just sat down in my apartment and wrote another poem entitled "You are me."

> Who are you?
> Why is this ending only a beginning?
> My mind can hear you
> My mind devastated by your desire

You cannot change
I cannot sustain
Go away, oh, God, go away.
Tell me that your sunset will restore my sanity.
Die. I cannot
Bring me into the wilderness where I can discover your betrayal
But I know, I know the lie
I know your truth and I know my delusion.
You are me.

For some reason that I didn't understand, and don't really understand now (except for the idea of validation), I sent this poem to a publisher and it was accepted for publication. Before it was published, my editor asked me to write a few sentences to give context to the poem itself. "It is about the devastating effects of mental illness, how it can unknowingly invade your life, silently grow worse, take complete control of your mind, and make you a stranger to yourself. It is like a cancer … too late to recover and impossible to overcome … [but] I do hope that it [the poem] is the first step on the path to recovery." The last sentence was a blatant lie. I wasn't recovering from anything — yet.

In February of 2007, I was living in a psychological wasteland. No friends. No money because I had blown it all on alcohol, drugs, and women. No career because the one I had chosen was so repugnant to my ideals. Just a piece of shit — if I blew my brains out, nobody would flinch. I have to say, I almost didn't hate myself anymore because there was no "self" to hate. I didn't feel like a person. I didn't feel alive. I didn't feel like I was a conscious actor in a world where we have free will to determine our destiny. I had even lost the ability to feel anything. Maybe the inability to feel was actually a feeling in itself — being a stranger on the outside, looking in at a world wondering why and how people were so fucking happy. I never did understand happiness, either as a concept in itself or as a state of being. How could people be happy if they really confronted the realities of life? If they did, there would be no room for happiness, unless, of course, a person was capable of one of the most sophisticated forms of self-denial that has ever existed. The thing I realized is that people don't think about this shit. Instead, they distract themselves with food, drink, drugs, marriage, sex (both extramarital and pre-marital), kids, 9-5 jobs, money pursuits, nice clothes, fancy cars, and rewards and accomplishments that have nothing to do with merit.

Yet, they are happy and I am a miserable fuck. So who wins in the end? They do. I can contemplate the big philosophical questions even though my reasoning capabilities can never possibly know the true nature of existence. I can feel angry, hurt, and betrayed, but that leaves me feeling depressed and alone. Those who don't think about these questions, who love baseball, plan their Saturdays around college football, and throw surprise parties for a partner's 30th anniversary, they make me look like a fool. I may think more, but they do more, and they do it so much better that the paradox kills me. Some people just look forward to every moment in their lives. For me, I never felt like there was a tomorrow. It was all just the same day. In fact, it was all the same second.

Then it all stopped. There was an area where I would never get "fired." There was an area no longer filled with cocaine and crack. There was an area with no connections, where nobody could break my heart and dehumanize my existence. There was an area that nobody could get to: my body. I owned my body. No one, and I mean no one, could tell me what to do or how to treat my body. My parents and friends could say whatever they wanted to say, but I had my body, which was untouchable. My girlfriends could fuck other guys but they couldn't change how I treated my body. My body was the one possession that stood apart from the pain and suffering; it stood apart from everything that was wrong yet still kept within it everything that was right. In early 2007, I became even more determined to make myself smaller. My self-esteem would rise and fall on my ability to successfully put something in the mirror that I liked. This was my time. It was my time for revenge. I included myself among the victims of that revenge.

I was now at the end of a long road while simultaneously beginning a new journey. My thinking had changed. I didn't care about health. Exercise was not an end in and of itself. I wanted to be thin. I wanted to be very thin. For the first time, the word "anorexia" appeared in the back of my mind. I didn't greet it with hostility, but with caution. At this point, I cared less about labels than I did about dropping as much weight as fast as possible. I actually drafted a plan to become super-skinny. For motivation, I visited several "pro-anorexia" sites on the internet. I'd heard about these a few years before while watching a show about eating disorders. I went to several "pro-Ana" websites and found a wealth of information, including lists of food with their accompanying caloric content and special diets that would melt the pounds away fast. I also discovered how to effectively "starve" your body and eat foods that would raise your metabolism and induce weight loss. Perhaps my favorite part of the "pro-Ana" websites was the "thinspiration" page, where you could see many pictures of anorexics with bones sticking out of nearly every part of their body. This served as motivation for me to keep losing and losing. I wanted my ribs to bulge out from my body. I wanted my skin to sag. I wanted to look gaunt and malnourished. I wanted to look like death.

The next time I went to Bally's I got back on the scale and it was sort of like the first day of school. Now that I was committed to being thin at all costs, I had to get my weight down as quickly as possible. When I stepped on the scale I weighed 152 pounds, just one pound less than several days before. It didn't really bother me that much. Yes, I wanted to be super-skinny and stick-thin. Thus, although my weight was only "normal," I knew that I would slowly but surely take the pounds off. The bottom line was that I was in control, and that's what I needed most at that point.

I don't want to say the weight loss happened gradually, though, because it didn't. Everything, including my weight, began to spiral downwards. In March, every morning I woke up and forced myself to go to Bally's. Whether I wanted to or not was irrelevant. I made a promise to myself that I would never, ever leave that place without burning at least 1,000 calories on the elliptical machine. I was true to my word. I would get on that machine and if, after an hour, I was twenty-four calories below 1,000, I'd restart the program to get twenty-four more. Unfortunately, although I didn't want to acknowledge this, we all know that these machines can be extraordinarily inaccurate. I heard that they could record a calorie burn 40% higher than that which was actually expended.

So I had to find a solution to this frustrating problem. I mean, you bust your ass, and then you find out that you've burned about 400 calories less than what you thought? Not a big deal. I would just go to the gym twice a day. The plan was to burn 1,000 calories every morning and then assume that the actual estimate was 40% higher than it should have been. In other words, even though I burned "1,000" calories, I only really burned 600. So I would go home, have a meager lunch, and then go back to the gym and burn off the extra 400 calories that the elliptical inaccurately calculated on my first run-through in the morning. Then the question came up — well, if the fucking machine is inaccurate, then it's inaccurate when you're burning either 1,000 calories or 400 calories! I felt so fucked. I had no idea how many calories I was burning and I was pissed at the uncertainty.

So, I just resorted to simplicity. I would ride the elliptical machine twice a day, for one hour each time, for a total of two hours. In doing so, the elliptical would calculate that I was burning over 2,000 calories, but, shit, even if it was inaccurate, I was still burning a lot of calories. There was proof of this because the next time I stepped on the scale, I was down to 149 pounds. When I saw this number, I didn't feel happy or celebrate. I was dead serious. I wanted to lose more — quickly. I wanted to lose as much weight as I possibly could. I have to say that this was the point where my anorexia was knowingly born. My weight loss was reversing the feelings of self-hatred and replacing the shame with a sense of self worth. Most of all, I was, for the first time in my life, gaining control over something very important to me. The number on the scale no longer became a number — it became a status symbol.

When I saw that number — 149 pounds — I was still within the normal weight range for my height (145-157). To me, being in the "normal' range meant I was "overweight" like everybody else. It represented failure. It represented not being "good enough." There was so much more weight to lose.

That week, when I saw my mom, she started noticing. In a worrisome tone, she said things like, "you look thin" or "don't lose any more weight." I loved every word. It made me want to jump right back on the elliptical. Guess what? Who was in control now? Me. The legal profession, the girl who had betrayed and fucked me over, the therapist, were all in the past. No more disappointment. No more sadness. It was all about power now, and I had it. I had control over whether I lost or gained weight. I had control over when, and how many times, I went to the gym. I had control over how much weight I wanted to lose and nobody could stop me. I was in control and there was nothing that anybody could do about it. Everybody was at my mercy now, and there was no way in hell that I was going to give this up. I could kill myself if I wanted. My life was now the ultimate *fuck you* to everyone else who said *fuck you* to me. I'm not changing — not now — not ever.

I woke up the next morning and walked proudly to the gym. My clothes were fitting more loosely and I was the master of my made-up universe. As I walked in, I purchased two bottles of those crazy energy drinks that are designed to increase your metabolism and help burn more calories during the workout. Of course, only one bottle is recommended, but that's for normal people. I'm not normal. I did my hour on the elliptical machine, going as fast as I could, looking like a total maniac in front of everyone else, and constantly monitoring my heart rate to get it as high as I possibly could. The hour ended and I had my typical 1,000 calorie burn, but then I thought, *why not do it again? You have no job, no girlfriend, and no life. You are a loser.* Actually, I did have a life — the one I was creating. So I rode the elliptical for another hour, burning another 1,000 calories. It felt great yet horrible at the same time. I was happy about the calorie burn, but my body felt like shit. I had to sit down on one of the benches near the exit, praying that I wouldn't faint or go into a seizure. Ultimately, everything turned out fine, especially my weight. I was down to 145 pounds. When I hit 145, the first thing that came to my mind was: 135. 125. 115.

I kept thinking to myself, though, that there must be more effective ways to burn a lot more calories. Realistically, 2,000 calories (according to the elliptical machine) a day was fine, but I wanted a workout even more intense. I started doing some online research. I perused all of the prominent health and fitness sites, the bodybuilding forums, and even the common sites like msnbc.com. When I did this, I discovered that I could, and should, be burning more calories a day if I just tweaked my workout in two ways. The first was through interval training. Basically, interval training means that, when you are walking, running, cycling, or whatever, you spend brief periods exerting yourself at maximum capacity. These intervals can range from twenty seconds (beginners), to two minutes (advanced) or more. The goal is to increase your heart rate so high that it continues to beat at a higher pace all day, thus burning more calories at rest. It is called the "after burn." I felt so happy to find yet another method for my weight-loss toolbox.

My research also revealed that intense and unstoppable weight training (for about thirty minutes) would greatly facilitate weight loss. Essentially, this requires you to do various exercises on all of the different nautilus machines, and after you are done with a certain number of repetitions on one machine, you sprint to another machine and begin doing a different exercise, and so on. Those thirty minutes are brutal — bench presses, chest presses, leg extensions, calf raisers, punch-ups, sit-ups, and the like. At first, it was exhausting, especially for that crazy fuck (me) who worked out on the elliptical machine for an hour, burning 1,000 calories, and then did the weight training. What a sick son-of-a-bitch, right? No way. I had created my own little world where nothing existed except me and my narcissism. I was the center of my fake universe, in control of everything, and impervious to anyone who dared to try to take "me" away from me. The scale was the God of my universe, and now read 140 pounds. No longer at "normal" weight. At this point I may not have been "anorexic" by technical standards, but the desire to control — and lower — my weight was now complete. I had an eating disorder. I knew it, and I was proud as hell of it. I was no longer a law student or a lawyer. I was no longer Erica's boyfriend or Amy's lover. I couldn't be labeled anymore. I was just me. Soon, though, I would want more. I didn't just want an eating disorder. I wanted the medal for being anorexic.

If I wanted to go below 140 pounds, which would cause me to be significantly underweight, I needed to make my workouts even more intense. This wasn't a problem because I had all the time I wanted. I had completely isolated myself from the world, including my family and friends (of which I had only a few left). In fact, by this time I had also eliminated from my life the few people with whom I was in contact, except for the limited conversations I had with Amy. I sat in my apartment alone, all day, every day. It was my sanctuary away from people and from all of the hurt, shame, and blame that I had placed on myself for everything that had gone wrong. The only time I left my apartment was to get a small amount of food or engage in intense exercise. However, I started to notice a problem. I wasn't exercising enough because I was at home for too long. There was this large space of time where I did nothing. So I started a new plan, and it was premised on that whole interval training idea, namely, that intense bursts of energy can have the effect of raising your metabolism for the rest of the day.

Upon waking in the morning, I would almost uncontrollably sprint between the walls of my apartment, which were about thirty feet apart from each other. I ran as fast as humanly possible, going back and forth so many times, and stopping only once I felt exhausted. Then I would immediately go to the bottom steps of my apartment (I lived on the second floor) and run up and down the stairs as many times as I possibly could. After that, I backed up against the wall of my bedroom, and squatted down so that all or most of my weight was placed on my legs. I stayed in this position until my legs were burning so much that I could not stand it any longer. Then, I picked up my 5-pound hand weights and started doing lunges across my apartment. After the lunges, I would take one of my chairs from the kitchen, and, with weights in each hand, proceed to step up onto the chair, one leg at a time. I would then go back to sprinting, running up the stairs, squatting against my wall, and finishing with jump-roping. This workout only lasted about 20-25 minutes because the activity was non-stop with no resting period between each exercise. I could feel my heart beating wildly after this workout, and I used to call it "setting the metabolic stage for the day." I had already started the fat-burning process with a beautiful caloric expenditure, and still had the entire day ahead of me to burn more calories.

After I finished my morning craziness, I would make coffee because the caffeine provided a bit more of a metabolism boost. I also made green tea, because my research revealed that the ingredients in green tea increased metabolism and supported weight loss. Finally, I would put cayenne pepper in both my coffee and tea, because the intense spice further increased my metabolic rate. It didn't matter that it made the coffee and tea taste terrible. Taste and other sense-experience doesn't serve as an obstacle when you are hell-bent on weight loss. If it would make me lose weight, then I would do anything.

My day started precisely the way I wanted: the calories were burning, the fat was melting, and the weight was dropping. It was only ten o'clock in the morning. What now? Walking. I decided to take up walking for a few reasons. First, walking burns a good deal of calories, especially when done over a long period of time. Second, it allowed me to leave my apartment and walk in the beautiful parks where I lived, which I found peaceful and comforting after the turbulent times I had experienced. Nature can be comforting in so many ways. Third, well, there is no third, except a re-emphasis of the first — it burns calories. So, as someone in the middle of a nervous breakdown, I put my black trench coat on, with my black hat, and just started walking and walking. I looked like a deranged serial killer. I walked everywhere. I walked through the parks. I walked through my downtown area. I walked through different towns. I walked for hours and hours, and only stopped when I felt satisfied that my pedometer had recorded enough steps to give me a good workout. One day I walked 30.26 miles.

After walking, I went to Bally's for a good hour of calorie burning. Then, I was done for the day. Except for my visit to the scale, which now read 138 pounds. It was such a life-affirming moment. I wasn't incompetent or incapable of success. I could accomplish something on my own. I wasn't worthless. I had control over something that made me feel successful, empowered, and passionate. Nobody was going to take that away from me.

After my first, grueling, all-day workout, I ordered a salmon salad from Chili's, which was one of my favorite chain restaurants. The meal was very good, at least by my parochial standards. I had now lost 90 pounds, and my eating habits were somewhat similar to those that I adopted when I initially started losing weight. I hadn't yet adopted the dieting techniques from the "pro-Ana" websites. I simply made better food choices, such as fish, chicken, and other lean meats. I also made sure to limit my intake of simple carbohydrates, and instead had a steady intake of whole grains, oatmeal, and other sources of complex carbohydrates. In addition, I stopped drinking soda and juice, and eliminated any fast food or foods containing excessive amounts of salt or fat. Any sweet foods, as much as I loved them, were also eliminated. Perhaps the biggest change in my routine was that I started to consume more fruits and vegetables with my lunches and dinners, and that made me feel both healthy and energetic. Basically, it was like I was building my own house with my body — regulating it with exercise and fueling it with the necessary nutrients.

Then I came to an important realization. I asked myself, *how the fuck am I going to lose more weight if I keep shoving all of these calories in my body?* I was consistently losing weight, but my appetite for further weight loss was insatiable. I wanted more and I wanted it now. Slow or gradual weight loss was not an option. I needed to find a better way of eating less, and of cutting the shit out of the calories I was eating. Exercise was only one half of the equation. To keep shrinking, I needed some way to change my diet so that my body could stop eating food and start eating itself. So I embarked on what I called the "elimination phase:" food was the enemy, and needed to be arrested and imprisoned, save for a few innocent bystanders.

I researched and studied every diet plan that existed, both conventional and alternative. None of them impressed me. They were either too complicated, unrealistic, or just unhealthy. For me, it was simple. Weight loss is based upon mathematics. You lose weight when you burn more calories than you consume. Thus, all of these shit diets, with their strategies, weekly weigh-ins, deprivations, and misrepresentations, all masked this simple mathematical formula. When you burn 3,500 more calories than you consume, you lose one pound. That is why weight loss should happen gradually over time, and not quickly or in a dangerous fashion. Also, it should be based not on a diet, but on a lifestyle change, a commitment to better eating habits that you can sustain for the rest of your life. Unfortunately, however, I wasn't interested in the dangers of fast or unhealthy weight loss. I wanted to lose weight now, and lots of it, because when I looked in the mirror, I still saw a fat, self-hating piece of shit. I would grab various parts of my body to reinforce my belief that there was still so much fat to lose. I wanted to disappear — literally. The mirror was both my enemy and salvation.

So I kept trying to formulate an eating plan that would rip the weight off me. I wanted to lose so much weight that I would be unrecognizable to my family and friends. I went back to the "pro-Ana" websites where there were specific "tricks" that you could use to make your body "feel" full without consuming any calories whatsoever. For example, the first rule of thumb was to drink as much water as possible. That would create a "fullness" feeling and delay the need to eat. It's called "water-loading" (no, not "water-boarding"). Then the website had its "food" section, where it would explain how to "restrict," that is, how to consume as little calories as possible each day.

For example, one trick is to take two bites out of an apple every half hour because that would signal to your body that it was being consistently fed, although in fact it was being starved to death. Also, you could eat as much celery as you wanted and, God forbid, if you had a binge eating episode (which is common when the body is in starvation mode), then you had your emergency kit of purging materials, whether it be ipecac syrup to induce vomiting, enemas, laxatives, fiber pills (you'd consume the whole bottle), or just exercising all day, every day, for the next few days while restricting your eating. I loved all these tricks and used them to aid in my weight loss attempt. What I loved most was the "thinspiration," namely, those pictures of anorexic men and women. To me, it represented my destination and destiny.

My eating disorder was now full-blown and starting to affect my health. I was beginning to feel very weak. I was tired very often. When I went into the shower, I began to have problems lifting my arms. Sometimes I felt like I was going to faint. I didn't care. I wanted the diet that would keep shedding the pounds. Eventually, based upon both my research and visits to the "pro-Ana" sites, I found an even better diet. It was so simple that I was shocked I didn't think of it myself. It was called the negative-calorie diet. The idea is simple. For certain foods, it takes the body more energy (calories) to digest them than are actually in the foods themselves. Thus, when you eat these foods, you are actually consuming "negative" calories. I struck gold. I was particularly happy because I had just started a journal in which I, among other things, listed the types of food and ingredients, i.e., spices, jalapeno peppers, etc., that had the effect of raising metabolism. So now I could combine negative calorie foods and metabolism-igniting ingredients to cause sudden and dramatic weight loss. The puzzle was coming together. The question then became, what foods are thought to have "negative" calories? My research did not take long. The list was as follows:

Fruits

Apple
Cranberries
Grapefruit
Lemon
Mango
Orange
Pineapple
Raspberries
Strawberries
Tangerine
Apricot
Blackberry
Blackcurrant
Guava
Honeydew Melon
Cantaloupe
Peaches
Plums
Watermelon
Papaya
Pineapple
Prunes

Vegetables

Asparagus
Aubergine
Beet
Broccoli
Cabbage (green)
Carrot
Cauliflower
Celery
Chili peppers
Cucumber
Dandelion
Endive
Garden cress
Garlic
Green beans
Lettuce
Onion

Radishes
Fennel
Gourd
Leek
Chicory
Marrow
Spinach
Tomatoes
Turnip

I finally discovered an exercise and eating plan that could get me where I needed to be: skeletal. I wanted my bones to protrude through my flesh. It would be my expression of all the anger and hurt that had gone ignored for so long. Death didn't scare me. People scared me. Life scared me. A life without anorexia, which I now called "Ana," scared me. A life without my exercise scared me. I had just escaped from a world that I found terrible and disillusioning. I could never go back. In many ways, I already felt like there was no going back.

I loved this diet. I could eat anything and everything off this list and not worry nearly as much that I would gain weight. Basically, I would be stuffing myself with vegetables and water every day. The "negative calorie" lifestyle would give me the weight loss I wanted and, more importantly, needed. I remember writing this "formula" into my journal, which read as follows:

> Early morning intense bursts of exercise ("compulsive exercise phase") + several hours of walking ("duration phase") + one-hour on the elliptical machine at Bally's (intense exercise for weight loss phase") + negative calorie foods (the "elimination phase") = *Ana* (that was my name for her — I wanted to give anorexia a name because I wanted to have a personal relationship with it. I have an eating disorder but not anorexia — yet.

There were some days when I didn't follow this plan, simply because I was physically unable to complete each step, or because I decided that just one of the steps would be ok for a day or two. I was burning massive amounts of calories and my eating disorder was my best "friend," with Ana waiting at the final destination. As part of my negative calorie diet, I would go to the local supermarket and buy bags of broccoli, carrots, and cauliflower, all mixed together. Each bag was fairly significant in size, but they were only one hundred calories each. So I purchased about five of them, and proceeded throughout the grocery store with my negative calorie list in hand. The majority of my food consisted of vegetables, and I made it a point to purchase the spiciest sauces at the store, so that I could dip my vegetables in it and give myself a metabolism boost. It didn't matter that the food would probably burn a hole in my mouth when I ate it. If it would burn through the fat, then I could handle anything. I needed to handle it, because I could still grab sections of fat on my body. I wished I could have taken a knife and just cut them off. Sadly, I would have to settle for starvation.

As I walked down the produce aisle, I found specific "dipping" sauces that would enhance my metabolism while eating: jalapeño and habanero peppers. I also included some cayenne pepper to sprinkle over my broccoli, carrots, cauliflower, lettuce, spinach, tomatoes, and all of the other vegetables that my body would have one hell of a time burning. I loved the whole concept of the negative calorie diet because the vegetables would make me feel "full," while the spices would speed up my metabolism. It was a win-win situation. It was also a lose-lose situation as far as my weight was concerned.

Then I went to the fruit section and found my new negative calorie friends. I purchased raspberries, strawberries, oranges, grapefruits, lemons, blackberries, and so on. What looked healthy inside my shopping cart was really the manifestation of a deadly illness taking a stronger hold on me. I was starting on the path of eliminating as many foods as I could from my diet. Only certain foods would now have access to my body, and only in certain quantities. It was certainly expensive, but money was no object. If I had to take money from my savings to lose the weight, then that would be fine. I would literally give my life to lose weight, but at this point, I didn't mean it literally.

I was the gatekeeper. Whatever food posed any threat to my weight loss efforts was eliminated. I stopped eating meat and became a vegetarian. I eliminated all dairy products. I was now a vegan. The only foods that were permitted to enter my body were negative calorie foods and "vegetable" burgers, which would provide a good yet low-calorie protein source. I might even allow protein bars, but that was it. I also discovered other ingredients and supplements that would make me skinny, and they included: Guarana, Yerba Mate, L-Carnitine, Thyroid Enhancers, and Conjugated Linoleic Acid (CLA), which are designed, generally speaking, to prevent your body from storing fat. Food represented everything that had gone wrong with my life. It could make me fat. It could make me ugly. It could confirm everything that I thought was wrong with me. I had to starve myself without literally starving myself. My food restriction came very quickly, and it was becoming complete.

However, for me, and for many other anorexics, the idea of "restriction" is not just limited to food. It also encompasses what we call "triggers." People, places, and things can all act as triggers. In essence, "triggers" are events or people that have caused us terrible pain, hurt, and shame in the past, which affect our ability to exercise control, psychologically and physically, in the present moment. They can cause us to engage in binge-eating episodes, self-harm, or other dangerous behaviors. Such behaviors result from the fact that we cannot deal with the emotional issues that arise when recalling various traumatic events in our lives. Thus, the self-destructive behavior allows us to suppress our feelings and channel our behavior in a different, albeit destructive direction. Triggers may come in many forms, such as the sight or smell of our favorite food, a visit from an ex-girlfriend who broke our heart, or a conversation with a family member about a traumatic event. Due to their disruptive and damaging nature, anorexics need to be very careful about what they do, where they go, and who they see. Most importantly, there can be no disruption of our sacred weight-loss routine. For me, triggering events would often result in a "binge" eating episode, where I would consume thousands of calories of food in one sitting. This was my worst nightmare, because it brought back not only the fear of weight gain, but all of the underlying feelings of failure, self-hate, rejection, and worthlessness. As I would find out later, binge-eating was not only a response to triggers, but also my body's defense against death by starvation.

In my case, nobody had the right to talk about my weight, appearance, or physical condition. Nobody was allowed to even think about bringing food into my apartment. I was proudly starving myself. If anyone tried to help me, they would be eliminated from my life. Anorexia was bringing me respect, self-worth, and success. I had no emotions anymore. I had lost the ability to feel. I was too consumed in my little anorexic world to feel the pain of the past or the dangers that might lie ahead. I was finally living my life. Fuck everybody else. I'm in control and if you try to threaten my world, you'll never see me again, and if you do, maybe I'll be dead.

Chapter Twelve

The Commitment to Anorexia

The Child Needs a Helping Hand

I was open to eliminating everyone from my life. At this point, I was 5'8" and 138 pounds, which is not that thin. I was not satisfied. I was not fat, but I still "felt" fat. Of course, since I come from an Italian family, nobody is considered "fat" unless they are almost obese. Thus, when I was fat, my parents never really saw me as fat. However, when I was 138 pounds, they saw me as anorexic, even though I was nowhere near that magic number. So, as my weight began to plummet, my mom began, all of a sudden, to become extremely concerned. She would drive forty minutes to my apartment and we would talk and talk and talk. She would tell me things like, "Adam, the last time people saw you, when you were at the house [my parents' house], they thought you looked sick." I took that as a compliment.

She remarked how pale I was and how the black circles under my eyes looked terrible. Then she made the biggest mistake you can make with anyone suffering from an eating disorder. She started discussing my food intake. She wondered why I was eating bag after bag of raw vegetables and eating raw blueberries out of the containers within which they were stored. She wanted to understand why I refused to let her take me out to dinner and why I seemed so preoccupied with food. Then at one point she said, "Adam, you have an eating disorder." Now, anorexics are amazing manipulators because they will do anything and everything to protect their eating disorder from outside, disruptive influences. So I responded by acting as if I was insulted by the question and said, "Of course not, Mom, I'm just eating healthier." What an outright lie. She thought this was a satisfactory explanation, probably because she wanted to believe it. All I needed for the moment was to keep my secret life intact and shut everyone out. I knew if I let anyone in, they would try to suck me back into the world I'd left behind.

My days thereafter weren't really "days," but kind of like the continuation of one long day that never ended. My three-part exercise regimen was in full force, and more like a torture session. I woke up and immediately began the various exercises that set my metabolism on fire. Then I made coffee and green tea, both sprinkled with cayenne pepper. I even added a cigarette to the mix, both for its metabolic and appetite suppressing qualities. Then I began the "duration" stage with my pedometer, tracking every step and mile that I walked. I never had a specific destination in mind, but I had a specific goal that must be reached: at least 20,000 steps. After a while, people started to recognize me. I was the crazy guy in the black clothes, walking in a maniacal state, who must be suffering from some mental disorder. I'm sure it certainly appeared that way. Well, it was that way. I was losing touch with reality.

Then it was time for lunch. Lunch was very simple for me. I would eat two bags of raw vegetables (broccoli, cauliflower, and carrots), or I might deviate and eat something else from the negative calorie list. Then I would have some vegetable burgers, which were high in protein but alarmingly low in calories and that other villain, carbohydrates. After lunch, usually around 2:00 p.m., I would start writing in my journal because I discovered that writing my thoughts, feelings, and whatever else was very therapeutic. I found that it really helps to allow your emotions and feelings to extend outward rather than inward, where they can metastasize and cause you to sink lower into depression. I'm not sure if the journaling was a subconscious attempt to begin the healing process, or a conscious attempt to document and reinforce my sense of anorexic accomplishments.

One day I remember writing in my journal that I had walked 42,945 steps, which is equivalent to 27.78 miles, in 5 hours, 42 minutes, and 42 seconds. After journaling, I would usually engage in some type of meditative exercise, both for its calming effects and for how it allowed me the ability to remain centered and at peace with myself. Sometimes it worked, and sometimes it was a disaster. There were moments when I couldn't bear the pain of thinking about things that I had done, or that were done to me. It was just too difficult, because I didn't see myself as a victim; I blamed myself, rightly or wrongly, for the events that caused my hatred of both the world and myself. I knew that I would eventually have to confront the traumatic experiences, as well as the emotional issues underlying my feelings of inadequacy and low self-esteem. I wasn't ready to re-visit that world, though, because if I did that, my bond with anorexia might be threatened. I would never take that chance because I needed Ana so much. She protected me from that reality. She made me feel loved and back in control of my life.

After miles and miles of walking, I would go to Bally's around 5:00 p.m. for my 1,000 calorie burn. Then it was on to the short but intense weight-lifting machines. I have to admit, though, that my interest in the weight-training portion of the workout was quickly waning. I never did, and still do not, enjoy weight training, and it was only a short time thereafter that I eliminated it from my evening calorie burn. At night, it was just me and the elliptical. To be honest, after the morning craziness and afternoon walking, an hour on the elliptical was quite enough exercise for me. I mean, fuck, I exercised for nearly six hours a day and ate raw vegetables.

As much as I didn't want to, I "had" to eat dinner. Eating was always a dangerous proposition. It meant calories and calories meant fat. Fat meant failure. Failure meant self-hatred. I did, however, have a plan. My food choices were carefully orchestrated. I knew the calorie content of everything in the supermarket. If I hadn't seen a particular product before, I almost always came within 10% of estimating the caloric content. Ultimately, I needed to ensure that, by the time I went to sleep, I burned about 1,000 calories more than I consumed for the day. With this in mind, I always started dinner off by drinking a lot of water so that I "felt" full. My appetizer was two bags of raw vegetables with the hottest sauce I could find. Then I would eat a few eighty-calorie each veggie burgers. These were the only foods allowed in my diet. Every day I ate the same meals.

However, what if I was still hungry after dinner? What would I do? I couldn't dare eat more food! Well, I found a convenient solution. It's common knowledge that foods high in fiber and/or protein help you feel fuller for a longer period of time. So, did I get foods with substantial amounts of fiber? Of course not. Instead, I purchased several bottles of fiber pills and after dinner I would shove some down my throat to stimulate the fullness feeling. If I woke up in the middle of the night feeling hungry, I would just dump about ten fiber pills in my system and go back to bed. The good part of this was that it helped me to stay within my rigid eating plan. The bad news is that it so fucked up my digestive system that I was in the bathroom more than I was in my bedroom.

In any event, I continued on my brutal 3-part exercise regimen every day, even on days when I was sick and exhausted. Amy called a couple of weeks later. I wasn't particularly nice to her and didn't want to see her. She was concerned. I didn't care. I just wanted her out of my fucking life. At that time, she represented everything that I wanted to leave behind. It was sad, actually. We did have wonderful times together. We did love each other. However, I was too consumed with losing weight to care. I was filled with resentment because I felt that she was dishonest and disloyal to me. So I made myself emotionally unavailable. I was in control, and I wanted her to go away and stay away. Unfortunately, I said some terrible things to her and for all of my days, I will regret them. I would yell at her, sarcastically, "No, I don't want to have lunch you…go home and be with your family." I also told her in one conversation, "Why do you want to come see me? Just go home and have sex with your husband!" Those and other comments hurt her in many ways, and I would not understand, until years later, how much they broke her heart. I'm sorry for what I said to her. She is a good person and genuinely cared about me. At that time, though, I was in a different place. I had another girlfriend — Ana.

Yes, Ana and I were getting along perfectly. I still stuck faithfully to my exercise plan, but for some reason (of course I should have known the obvious) I started to find it more and more difficult to complete my daily workouts. My morning torture session was an event that I began to dread. I liked walking, but it took hours and hours out of my day. While the elliptical machine was my favorite activity, I was suddenly having difficulty finishing the one-hour sessions. Deep down, I knew I was exercising too much, but I was in denial because I needed my marriage to Ana to become official. I needed to reach the "golden" weight that defines you as officially anorexic. I would earn the "anorexic" label if my weight fell fifteen percent below the lowest point of the normal range for my size. In doing the calculation, I had to reach a weight of 123.25 pounds. After doing my exercises the next day, I stepped back on the scale. The result was 130 pounds.

The scale was now my God. It controlled my mood, my emotions, and how I felt about myself. In other words, even though I finally felt that I had achieved control in my life, the scale actually had control over me. I didn't care though, because it was ok for me to feel in control and controlled at the same time. The eight-pound weight loss was an affirmation of my strength, resilience, perseverance, and courage. I loved the idea of starvation because it made my body look beautiful and, more importantly, it made me happier internally. I felt like an entrepreneur who single-handedly started up a business and then, over time, became wildly successful, had over 100 employees, and was living the dream life. I convinced myself that the worst days of my life were over. No more law practice. No more interaction with lawyers who thought they were doing something good when they were doing something meaningless. No more relationships with married women. No more interaction with a woman who decided to have a child with her husband while we were having an affair. No more drug abuse. No more hookers. No more phone sex. No more negative energy. I had instead built up, from nothing, a perfect body and an exercise program that even the most elite athletes would find challenging. I did it myself. I was proud of myself. But the fight was not yet won. I needed to lose more weight — fast.

Chapter Thirteen

Thinner and Thinner

I was now down to 130 pounds — what I weighed when I was twelve years old. While the old, three-step plan had worked up to this point, I was experiencing extreme fatigue and, on many days, not completing the workouts and obtaining the requisite caloric expenditure. On some days I didn't have the energy to walk to the bathroom to urinate, so I had to lie down on my couch, sleep, and use an empty water jug as my portable bathroom. I was beginning to shorten my walks and take long naps during the afternoon. Contrary to what I was thinking, my body had started slowing my metabolism as a defense mechanism against starvation. I came to the realization that I simply could not sustain my activity level anymore. However, I knew that I could maintain this level of activity if I did one thing: eat more. That simply wasn't a possibility.

All of this made me extremely nervous because without burning as many calories as I normally did, I was putting myself at grave risk for gaining weight. That scared me because my entire universe centered on weight loss. It was my last attempt at validation. If I gained a pound, it would mean that I had failed just like I did at my jobs and in my relationships. Weight gain represented everything that I hoped I was not, and it had the power to take everything from me. If I could not succeed in the world that I had created, then I couldn't succeed in any world. When I thought of weight gain, I thought of suicide. I would rather die than gain a pound.

My thoughts were irrational, as was I as a whole. I wasn't just a person with an eating disorder. I was a person with major depressive disorder who saw the world in a different way. To me, the world rewarded shallow, materialistic, selfish, and phony people who didn't have any sense of morals or values. The idea that we are here to "serve others" is so virtuous, but the opposite of the way people conduct their lives. The "haves" don't really help the "have-nots." Instead, the "haves" want more and more. They love to serve themselves, often at the expense of other people. Yet they receive recognition, and truly good people, who do, in fact, want to serve others, are often, but not always, left wondering where things went wrong. The sentimental statements that we use to define our persons and our professions are pure bullshit.

My weight loss, however, could not be more real. My most important goal up to this point in my life was to weigh 123.25 pounds. To me, that would be a momentous, life-time achievement. Most people would think I was crazy. *That's a good thing, though, because if they think I'm nuts, then I must be sane.* It didn't matter anyway because I didn't care about what anyone thought. I just wanted to control what they did. They could not hurt me anymore. They could not talk down to me. They could not control me. They could not see me the way they wanted to see me. I was trying to become a new person, but that couldn't happen until I became anorexic. My entire sense of self-esteem and self-acceptance depended upon my weight. It was the sole arbiter of whether I was good or bad, moral or immoral, respectful or disgraceful, good-looking or ugly, impressive or depressive, and constructive or destructive.

When I was thinking about how to venture down to the 123.25 mark, I made, given my physical condition, some initial decisions. First, I decided to stop walking. I was too weak and tired. The morning portion, however, was indispensable. As hard a workout as it was, the sheer intensity of pushing my body to its limits and igniting my metabolism was essential. The morning simply could not begin without this ritual. The question then became, what the fuck was I going to do between 9:00 or 10:00 in the morning and the time when I went on the elliptical (around 5:00)? I had no fucking idea. What I did know was that, without the walking, weight gain became a more significant possibility.

The first few days after I stopped walking, I started sleeping for several hours during the afternoon. I knew that my body needed the sleep, even though I was yearning, at every moment, to go outside and start walking again. I was in exercise-withdrawal. Compulsive exercise by anorexics is like a drug addiction, except that instead of physical withdrawals, I was stuck with almost unbearable emotional anguish. I felt like I was in a prison. If I had my way, I would exercise all day. However, I was too tired and my body would not respond. I felt like I was lying in a waiting room waiting for weight gain. Of course, the reason that I couldn't do what I wanted to do, was because of the thing I wouldn't do: eat food.

After a few days of not walking, I found myself in the middle of nowhere, both physically and mentally. I thought that I would feel better because of the rest, but that didn't happen. I became exhausted after my morning session. It took sheer will to go to Bally's and complete my elliptical workout. When I went into the shower and tried to wash my hair, I had to bring my head very, very low and close to my body because I could not reach my arms higher than my shoulders. My stomach always felt fucked up because I either never ate or ate voluminous amounts of raw vegetables. It didn't help that I was sometimes ingesting ten or fifteen fiber pills in a single day. Yet, I remained stubborn. I refused to listen to my body, which was telling me that it was time to end all of this nonsense. I was either in denial or would rationalize why I needed to continue down the path towards Ana. *After all, I'm only 5'8" and 130 pounds! That really isn't that skinny!! I need to find the energy somewhere, but not from food! I'm not even in the anorexic category.* I was just one of those "eating disorder not otherwise specified" patients, which essentially means you don't have the talent to starve yourself down to Ana's requisite weight. I didn't want to have a junior varsity eating problem.

No, that wasn't going to be me. I was not JV and would not fail to make the 123.25 destination. It was, for me, a matter of believing in myself, or believing the negative things that other people said or did to me over the years. It was time to step it up, rather than step it down. I made a mistake when I decided to stop walking. What the fuck was I thinking?! *Get your sorry, piece-of-shit ass off the couch, you worthless fuck, and start working even harder if you want to reach Ana.* So, in April of 2007, things went back to normal. Despite my fatigue, I resumed the 3-part exercise regimen. This time, though, I decided to walk around a small park in my town, largely because it was so beautiful and calming, and provided me with a sense of peace.

However, it was also next to the police station, and every day they were exposed to some guy in a black hat and trench coat walking feverishly around the park about 20-25 times. They must have thought I was crazy and, if there was some criminal law that I could have been charged with, I'm sure they would have been eager to throw me in jail. It was only when I began my recovery that my neighbors told me, in fact, that they thought I was not only crazy, but dangerous as well. Truthfully, I looked like a crazy person because I was a crazy person. I was also in the midst of a nervous breakdown. Those labels, or that perception, meant nothing to me. With 123.25 pounds now in sight, I walked hard, fast, and furiously around that park because the only thing on my mind was burning calories. I think my appearance shocked many people. Once when I went to the grocery store to get my "negative calorie" foods, the manager asked me, as I was walking out, to show him my receipt, as if I was blatantly stealing vegetables in plain sight. I didn't even contemplate stealing. I wasn't contemplating anything at all except weight loss. I needed to lose seven more pounds. Then the next time I went to Bally's, I received very bad news — the scale read 132 pounds — a two-pound weight gain.

I was in shock. I had been working out nearly six hours per day. How could I have gained weight?!?! This could not be happening! Well, it was happening. I went from 130 to 132 pounds in one week. Then I came to the realization, however irrational, of why I had gained the weight. Remember when I was so tired that I stopped the walking portion of my exercise and basically sat on my couch, slept, and pissed in an empty gallon water jug? Well, because of that, I thought, I had decreased my caloric expenditure so exponentially that I was losing ground. The reason why I stopped walking (the pure exhaustion), I decided, was an absurd excuse not to continue with my daily exercise. *Tired? Fuck you, Adam. Suck it up.* When I saw 132 pounds, my self-esteem took such a hit that I felt like I had lost control. The scale was the parent and I was the child. And Ana was drifting away, just like "Wilson" did in *Castaway*.

I wasn't going to let this happen. At thirty years old, I needed something positive to happen. I needed to believe in me again. Yet, there was part of "me" that was becoming the enemy. I was 15 pounds underweight, and I could feel that my body was doing everything it could to put the weight back on. I wasn't just going through an emotional struggle; I was going through a physical struggle. I knew that my body was starting to employ various mechanisms to bring me back to a normal weight, and that scared the shit out of me. I recalled all of those statistics about dieting, such as the fact that 95% of diets fail and most people not only gain all of their weight back, but 10% more. So now my body was working deliberately against me, putting me 8.75 pounds away from Ana. The 2-pound weight gain was threatening to take control from me. If I lost this battle I would kill myself. And I meant it.

All I needed was 8.75 pounds. I thought of anything and everything to get the weight off. I could increase my interval training. I could jog instead of walk. I could stay on the elliptical for two hours instead of one. I could increase the duration of my morning exercise and torture myself by running up and down the stairs fifty times. I didn't like these ideas because I was tired of doing the same shit over and over again. Out of sheer luck, however, I found a much better solution. When I was on one of my walks during late April, I walked by a yoga studio. I had never been a proponent of yoga. Although I knew nothing whatsoever about it, I had the audacity to form the opinion that it was for weak people. I thought, all you do is put yourself in these odd positions, like the Kama Sutra, and then after about an hour of looking like an idiot, you go home. It's really not a workout, I thought, because you don't break a sweat, you burn like five calories, and then you go home feeling like you've done something positive for your body even though you've probably fucked it up because of putting it in all of those uncomfortable and unnatural positions.

Despite these ignorant assumptions, I decided to do some research to examine whether my assumptions were correct and/or if I could benefit calorically from such a workout. The first thing I discovered was that there are many different types of yoga that are performed at varying degrees of intensity. There was, for example, Ashtanga Yoga, Iyengar Yoga, Bikram Yoga, and Power Yoga. Would any of these exercises help me reach my goal? Yes. Bikram Yoga. I discovered that Bikram was a specific type of yoga whereby you enter a room (with a "yoga mat") that is over 100 degrees Fahrenheit, and sometimes even higher. Then, the instructor proceeds to guide you through twenty-six poses which are meant to strengthen and stretch nearly every part of your body. These poses looked brutally hard and, in fact, mirrored some of the exercises that I did in my early morning torture session. So, I would be exercising in a room at or above 100 degrees, doing twenty-six grueling poses over a 90-minute period. This was exactly what I needed to reach Ana. There was, however, an obstacle. I wasn't sure whether the studio in my town offered that type of yoga. When I had walked by, I hadn't noticed the type and nature of yoga that was offered. So I anxiously walked back to the studio, and right on the front was a sign saying "Bikram Yoga offered here." The lights went on in my head. I had the solution to my 8.75 pound dilemma. This shit was going to melt away the pounds.

The next day I immediately purchased a yoga mat and signed up for a month's worth of Bikram Yoga. As my first session approached, I was both excited and nervous. *How the fuck am I going to handle intense exercise in 100 degree heat for an hour-and-a-half? What if I pass out?* I had no idea, but my fears were overridden by the amazing weight-loss prospects that this exercise had in store for me. When I arrived at the first session, I was instructed to take all of my clothes off except for my shorts and go into the yoga room with my mat and lie down face-up until the instructor came in to begin the class.

When I opened the door to the yoga room, I could not believe the intensity of the heat. It was like being put in an oven at 350 degrees. I started sweating almost immediately, which was a great sign. My emotions were a cross between ecstasy and fear. I knew that this might lead to the weight-loss breakthrough, but I also knew it might, figuratively speaking, kill me. I placed my yoga mat on the floor and sat down. The other people were lying down in a meditative state but I wasn't really comfortable doing that yet. I was dealing with the physical difficulty of the situation, which was something I had never experienced before.

After about ten minutes, the instructor came in and we were told to stand up and begin some basic stretching exercises. These were not difficult, but by this time I was sweating profusely, as were many of the other people. We then began the actual poses, and they were anything but easy. Some of them were designed to increase strength, such as one where we were instructed to do leg squats and hold the position for about thirty seconds. Then, we had to place our knees together and do the same squat, again holding for about thirty seconds. Not only were my legs burning, but the sweat was now flowing, not dripping, from my body. Then, we had to do a third set of leg squats where, after holding the position, we rose up in stages. It was so pleasantly miserable. My body was doing things that it had never done before, and I could envision the heat just melting me away. I started to see veins bulging out from my inner thighs, which was thrilling. When I looked in the mirror, I saw some, but not all, of my ribs. I was hoping that maybe I'd become skinny enough to be featured on the "pro-Ana" websites.

Anyway, the poses which focused on leg strength were not even the most difficult ones. During one pose I had to stand up, balance my body on one leg, and then lean forward with my arms directed straight towards the mirror. Aside from the difficulty in balancing, I could feel my heart racing as if it could not keep up with the energy that my body needed to get through the workout. Those were just three poses. There were twenty-six over the course of ninety minutes. By the time I finished my first session, I had the most awful headache I think I've ever experienced, which was due to serious dehydration. I must have consumed about 60-70 ounces of water after that session. I was also so draped in sweat that it looked as if I had come out of a rainstorm. I was dizzy and felt faint. I fucking loved it. This class burned more calories than anything else that I'd ever done. I couldn't wait to get back.

This session changed everything. No more walking. No more elliptical. Just my morning torture session and Bikram Yoga. It became so simple yet anything but simplistic. By the next day, my body was so sore that I didn't even do my morning workout routine. I was just too fucked up, but it was a good fucked up. I must have burned a million calories during that yoga session and, unlike that bitchy elliptical, there was no room for miscalculation. As tired as I was, I had the desire, in fact the need, to go to another class as soon as possible. Since I had taken the schedule with me the day before, I saw that there was a class at 10 a.m., so I got my yoga mat and headed to the studio. It was amazing. Even better than the first one. I didn't just simply do the poses this time. I did them with more intensity. I pushed myself harder. I wanted to sweat more. I wanted to burn those calories so that I had more bone than flesh. I wanted to see more veins. It was no longer that my self-esteem depended on Ana. It was my life. And I was in for a fight that was soon to test the limits of my physical and emotional capabilities.

Before I even knew of the struggle ahead, I remained faithful to my daily yoga sessions. After my first week, I knew that it was time to step on the scale. It was judgment day. Everything that I worked for, hoped for, and dreamed of came down to that moment. The world is a very large place, but for me it consisted of just a scale. I walked into Bally's and just sat there for a while doing nothing. I was scared. *What if the scale showed 132 pounds again? What if it showed 133 pounds? 135 pounds? How would I deal with this?* The truth was that I would not be able to deal with it. I was at the mercy of the scale. I knew that I had done everything possible to maximize my chances of victory. I was dehydrated. I had used two enemas to clear out my system. I took a host of fiber pills and, of course, I ate nothing before the weigh-in. The result? 127 pounds. 3.75 pounds away from Ana. I was ecstatic because I was winning again. I was doing something that very few people could do. I could starve myself better than anyone else. I was happy and proud of myself. I was about to belong to an elite, exclusive club of individuals whose bodies are a statement against everything that is wrong with the world.

The battle was not yet over. I still had almost four pounds to lose. Ana symbolized victory over everyone who had taken advantage of me throughout my life. This was not only my revenge, but my way of saying "fuck you" to the world, to those who always looked for what was wrong rather than what was right in me, to those who made me feel worthless and unworthy of love, to those who betrayed me, to those who never loved me unconditionally. I was on my victory lap and to get there, I decided to go to my yoga classes twice a day. That's right. I was exhausted but that didn't matter anymore. It was a living hell, but by increasing my caloric expenditure, I would reach my goal. The instructors complimented and praised me for my sheer determination and desire to "perfect" my yoga practice, but they knew nothing of what was really happening. I was in the final stages of my progress towards anorexia nervosa.

Sometimes, however, unexpected things occur that make you realize that you're in a more serious fight than you anticipated. It's hard to describe what happened. When I went to bed one night after a day filled with two yoga classes, I suddenly awoke in the middle of the night. I felt like a wild animal in search of its prey, a feeling like none I'd ever experienced. I found myself rushing out of my apartment like a crazed fool to the nearby 24-hour gas station. Once I got there, I bought two jars of peanut butter, Wonder Bread, grape jelly, about three pints of ice cream, and about sixteen Reese's Peanut Butter cups. Maybe I got more stuff. I really don't remember it all. What I do remember is that, as soon as I left the store, I began devouring these foods like a vulture. I simply couldn't put it in my mouth fast enough. I needed more and more. I stuck my hand in the peanut butter jars and just threw as much peanut butter in my mouth as I could. I was devouring the Reese's like those competitive eaters who take down hot dog after hot dog at their annual, disgusting eat-as-much as you can contest. My mouth was literally filled with food. It was as if I was consciously unconscious. When I went home, I made about five peanut butter and jelly sandwiches. I put so much peanut butter and jelly on them that I went through both jars and the jelly. Then I ate the rest of the Wonder Bread. Next it was the ice cream. I had chocolate chip cookie dough, caramel, and Reese's peanut butter cup ice cream. I ate as much of the ice cream as I could until I was so violently full that I almost vomited. My stomach was distended. I thought it was going to burst. My heart was racing. Maybe I should have vomited and purged all of this shit from my system. However, I hate vomiting and that was the one thing that I wouldn't do, even after a binge.

I was in a state of shock and confusion concerning what happened. *How did I lose control? What is happening here? How could I possibly eat this much food? Oh my God, my weight is going to skyrocket!* I felt so disgusting, not just physically, but emotionally. I hated myself for what I had just done. I hated myself for not having any control. I hated myself for failing. I hated myself for feeling so disgusting. I hated myself for being me. I felt like a criminal. What I didn't realize, but would soon, is that I'd had my first "binge-eating" episode, which is the body's defense against starvation. Fuck, I didn't care about that. I cared about what the scale would say the next morning. The scale responded appropriately: 135 pounds. I was mortified and wanted to slit my wrists or stick a gun in my mouth. How could I possibly gain eight pounds in one day?! Of course, I knew it wasn't "real" weight gain, but by looking at that number, I knew how quickly Ana could fall away from my grasp.

I needed to do things that would tighten her grasp around me. Emergency procedures were required immediately. I went to the local drug store and stocked up on enemas, diuretics, laxatives, fiber pills, and whatever else would purge this shit from my system. I took my goodies, went home, and began to try and fix the problem. The first were the enemas. I needed to do everything possible to bring down the weight. That wasn't enough. I ingested diuretics, because I needed to drain as much fluid as possible from my body. I also took laxatives and fiber pills, hoping for any and all elimination of the junk that I had put in my body. At this point, I could do nothing more but wait. I was still bloated and nauseous from the binge and simply couldn't garner up the energy to exercise. I had to simply sit and feel fat. It was horrible. I wanted so much to move, but my body wouldn't let me. I had "gained" eight pounds in one day and would have to go through living hell to get it back. Just wait, I thought, until my body feels a bit better. Then I can go out and purge the shit out of myself. I would exercise until my stomach was inverted and I could see bones again.

That's exactly what I did. By the early afternoon, I was able to exercise. This time the exercise would be more severe. I would punish myself for the horrible wrongdoing the night before, which had left me with feelings of shame, disgust, and self-hatred. I started with the torture session in my apartment. Then I started walking for hours. I walked fast and hard around town. After that I went to my evening yoga class. Between the enemas, laxatives, and diuretics, coupled with the exercise and fasting (I wouldn't even touch food), I thought I had minimized the damage. The scale would answer that question the next morning.

What was most important to me was that I went to sleep feeling back in control. I wanted simply to conclude that this was an aberration that would never again occur. Then it happened again. I binged. I woke up at 3:00 a.m., feeling so ravenous that I could not control my desire to run back to the gas station and stock up on as many sweet treats as they had in the fucking store. It wasn't much different than the night before. Ice cream, Dove chocolate ice cream bars, Snickers ice cream bars, chocolate chip cookie dough, Reese's Pieces, donuts, two jars of Skippy peanut butter, grape jelly, and Wonder Bread. I raced out of the store, got home, and began eating like a stone-aged human who underwent a famine and hadn't eaten in months. I was in a blind rage with food as the victim.

There was no method to the madness. I simply placed all of the food on my kitchen table and started eating everything in random order as fast as I could. It was like my last binge, but worse. It felt like I was in a state of unconsciousness. I just ate and ate and ate, until I could not any more. The emotional part was worse. How could I binge two nights in a row? I had just spent the previous twenty-four hours killing myself to get rid of the first binge, and then I did it again? I was losing control! My only purpose in life was caving in around me and it was entirely my fault. Ana was leaving me and there was nothing I could do about it. The only thing left in my world was starting to hurt rather than help me. I didn't want my eating disorder to confirm the worst that I thought of myself. Yet that's exactly what the binges did. At this point, I wasn't simply worried about gaining weight. I was scared that I would go insane.

I wanted to commit suicide at that moment. Only the fear of death, the fear of nothingness, stopped me. I already felt like a meaningless, pathetic, worthless fuck, as if I was both dead and alive at the same time. Then I just screamed as loud as I possibly could — the scream of a hopeless, desperate individual crying out for help. There wasn't anybody to help me. If I wanted Ana, I had to fight harder than ever. Yet something was going terribly wrong. My body was betraying me, just like Amy, just like everyone and everything else. I was split in half. My mind so desperately needed anorexia while my body was starting to fight me. I didn't know the difference between right or wrong. I could not even contemplate, or handle the fact that maybe my own journey in the eating-disordered world was destructive rather than constructive. Maybe it was all a mistake. Perhaps the true victory was letting go, rather than running toward, Ana. I had to shut these thoughts out. I could not accept that I had been under a delusion this whole time. I had emotionally invested so much of myself, and there was no way this too could be wrong. It was all I had left. Even if it was wrong, I had passed the point of no return. I needed 123.25, and would die trying if that was required. Unfortunately, things got worse when I put myself on the scale the next morning — 140 pounds. I was losing control, and losing the only thing that mattered to me.

I needed help and I knew it. I called my mom. She knew what I had been going through all along, but I had isolated everyone from my life by that point. When I called my mom I immediately started screaming over the phone. I wasn't saying anything. I was just screaming and crying. After my first episode, I had researched the idea of "binge eating" and discovered that anorexics commonly go through this as the body attempts to defend itself against starvation. That didn't matter to me. I needed to control any desires to binge so that I could lose more weight. My mom was extraordinarily concerned and came to my apartment. We talked and talked and talked. She would sleep at my apartment for days at a time. She took care of me. She massaged my aching muscles. She told me how skeletal I looked, and how she would help me through this because she loved me. She told me that I would get through this horrible nightmare. I hoped she was right. I wasn't sure if, at this point, I felt my eating disorder was a problem rather than a solution. What I did realize was that it was becoming more complicated.

Chapter Fourteen

The Struggle for Control

Something Beautiful Is Dying

My mom was very worried. As I went through one of my morning torture sessions, Mom watched in shock, saying that she thought I would have a heart attack. I didn't worry about heart attacks, low potassium levels, low blood pressure, anemia, or anything else. I wanted my reward. Sometimes we would go on walks together before I went to my yoga class. I didn't tell my mom about the daily enemas, laxatives, and fiber pills. We talked about almost anything. On several occasions I got very angry as I told her about the hurt and pain that I experienced during my life. I wasn't blaming her. I was purging from myself all of the negative feelings and sentiments that I had allowed to fester in me for so long. Many of them were directed at me, and my failure to take care of myself emotionally. For example, I was never assertive or good at drawing boundaries. I let people take advantage of and exploit me. Also, my idealism was shaken by people in the legal profession, by Erica, and by Amy. For years, I had allowed all the feelings of disillusionment, betrayal, and hurt to remain unspoken. I couldn't hold them inside any longer. I would scream at my mom, asking why things went so wrong, why things were so unfair, and why people sucked so much. I needed to get this out. I had harbored all of it for years. It made me feel better — sometimes. What really made me feel better is that I was now striking back and people were finally at my mercy.

Sadly, during these walks I said some horrible things to my mother and about my father, essentially blaming them for the things that were happening in my life. I made her cry. Of course, my parents were not responsible for what happened in my life. I was speaking from a point of anger and irrationality. As I look back, I'll never forget what I did. I'm sorry, Mom and Dad.

Despite how awfully I was acting, my mom listened. She cared. She didn't argue with me. She was supportive. Some people wouldn't have been. She was. I was lucky, especially considering my condition. One thing I can say is that when you have people who truly care about you, they will do anything to help you in times of need. My mom is a perfect example of that principle.

The days began to get very dark and dangerous. I was fighting to get to Ana, and, no matter how hard my mom tried, there was nothing she could do or say to stop me. Ironically, I needed anorexia to save my life. I needed to feel that I could accomplish something, anything. I was at the point in my struggle where it was now or never. I was physically and mentally exhausted. If I reached 123.25, I would have permanence; I would have the ultimate badge of honor, saying always and forever that I had made it, that I had done what so many people had tried to do and failed, or never tried at all. It was time to reach down as far as I could and give all of myself. My life was at stake, although I didn't realize that it was at stake in a much different way than I thought. Indeed, what I was pursuing as a positive goal was really a grave threat to my health.

My mom tried desperately to save me and to change my mind. She stayed by my side. She purchased book after book with me, talking about how deadly anorexia was and how lasting its effects could be on my body. She listened to all of the hate and anger that I felt about life, the law, people, and about myself. She pointed out everything that I had ever done that was positive in my life, such as graduating with a high grade-point average in college; graduating from law school with honors; getting a Master of Laws degree; publishing numerous law review articles; being a sensitive, honest person who was cared about by my family and friends; and being someone who was loved unconditionally by so many people. She purchased beautiful frames for my diplomas to highlight my achievements. She accompanied me, as an act of support, to my yoga sessions, even though she didn't enjoy it at all. She drove me forty minutes to a hospital where I had group therapy with other individuals (all women) with eating disorders. She joined a group of parents who had children with eating disorders. She told me how much she loved me again and again and again. She gave me anything I wanted. However, these external actions couldn't satiate the internal void. She couldn't give me what I really wanted, what I thought would fill that void — Ana.

Now it was time to pull out all the stops. In the midst of this, something incredible happened. I received a telephone call. I got the job. I would be a law professor starting in the fall. I had actually achieved one of my dreams. I would be standing in front of a classroom, teaching law students, and doing something that made me feel passionate and meaningful. It was like being born again. I could start over. I could begin again with a clean slate. I was happy at this news. Maybe, just maybe, I could get back a slice of idealism, or instill it in my students. Maybe I could be the teacher in law school that I never had. Maybe I could be an agent of change, and inspire people to pursue their passions in life, and serve others. However, as pleasant as it was to receive that phone call, I couldn't be happy because my sole source of happiness was eluding me. Everything would be ok if I reached my goal weight. Until then, everything was on hold. Out of self-perceived necessity, I was obsessed with being an official anorexic. I needed anorexia so badly. I would do anything — even sacrifice myself — in pursuit of that destination.

It was May. I would leave in early August to prepare for my new teaching job. I would be living in a different city that I knew nothing about. If I went there as a failed anorexic, then I'd probably wind up fighting for 123.25 while trying to master the art of being a good teacher. That would be a recipe for disaster. It was, however, more complicated than that. If and when I reached my goal weight, I would still want to maintain and continue to be an official anorexic. It wasn't as if I would suddenly decide to gain weight. In fact, I would probably want to lose more. So I had some serious issues going forward. Maybe I wouldn't be physically or mentally able to teach. Maybe I would be so consumed with weight loss that I would suffer serious health issues.

I didn't worry about that for the moment. I didn't even have anorexia yet. So I went into high gear. The final attempt. For the first time though, I felt fear. Deadly fear. I knew that my body was being pushed beyond its limits. There were times when I came home from yoga and felt so dizzy that I felt like I'd faint. The caloric deprivation was so severe that my binges increased to four or five times a week. On one occasion, I was stopped by a policeman and he took one look at me, and I could tell that he was taken aback by my appearance. I'm not sure if he thought that I was drunk or just physically compromised. That's when, for the first time, it hit me. Without any warning, I suddenly thought that maybe this struggle, which I would view as my crowning achievement, was the devil in disguise. I don't know how to describe it, but whether it was from exhaustion or desperation, something told me that I was, and had been, very wrong. This was not a game. There was no finish line. There was no victory, no reward at the end. After all was said and done, I would still be stuck with *me* and all of the feelings from which I sought so desperately to escape. The real victory would come from confronting my past traumas, dealing with the hurt and pain caused in my life, and learning to love, respect, and accept myself. When these thoughts came into my mind, I said to myself, *it's too late, I have to get there.* Even if I was playing a dangerous game, I couldn't stop. I thought that if I reached 123.25, I would feel true happiness.

Maybe Ana was like Sharon Stone from *Basic Instinct*. Maybe I'd get a good fuck but die in the process. Or perhaps I was afraid that 123.25 might not bring the validation that I so desperately sought. I don't know why I was, all of a sudden, contemplating the negative consequences that might befall me if I reached Ana. Unfortunately, it was too late to worry about the "why" because I had to focus on the "how." To turn back now would be to acknowledge that everything I'd invented was as fake as the world I'd left behind. I resumed the workout and, some days when I was on the elliptical, I was able to raise my heart rate to 172 beats per minute. I was taking serious risks with my health to get to a destination that was even unhealthier.

My mom often stayed with me for days. On one of our walks in the park I said to her, "Mom, if something does happen to me, I want you to know that I always loved you and that I do love you. And I want you to tell that to everyone else." She looked at me and said, "Son, I'm not going to let that happen." I guess somewhere, deep in that part of me where honesty still resided, I knew that I could die. I cared more about losing the weight than I did about dying.

My body was telling me to stop; my mind wouldn't let me. I would often stagger back to my apartment with no energy and just fall on my couch. When Erica decided to suddenly come to my apartment one afternoon, she said that I looked like a holocaust victim. That made me so happy. It motivated me to lose more weight. Yet, I could not ignore the physical effects that starvation and compulsive exercise were having on my body. My mom would rub my head, my back, and my legs when I could do nothing but lie on my couch. During this time, though, something more was going on. Truth was involuntarily and unwelcomingly entering my life.

I started to hate my exercise regimen and grow to dread the daily starvation. What was happening? Was I starting to realize that my dream of becoming an anorexic was actually a journey into a deadly nightmare? I didn't know. Was I starting to think that I had punished myself enough for the self-hatred that ran through my body faster than the most rabid form of cancer? I was slowly, almost unknowingly, changing, although I didn't want to change. I had come this far. I had to win. I needed to win. It was my last chance to find a reason to live. I had to shut the truth out.

So I kept on going. I got back on the scale. I was 128 pounds. Only 4.75 pounds to go. I could see the light at the end of the tunnel, but there was an obstacle in my way. I was binging too frequently. I simply could not stop it. I did everything I could. I tried to resist by taking sleeping pills. I went to my doctor, and he gave me Valium, so I tried to knock myself out before bed so that I would not wake up. Sometimes it worked. Sometimes I took the Valium in sufficient amounts that I didn't wake up. When I did, I was covered in my own urine. I didn't care. As long as I didn't binge, nothing else mattered. I prayed to God. Please let me make 123.25. Please God. As if there weren't more pressing problems in the world than my making it into the official "anorexia" club.

I pressed on and on in what I considered to be the final days of achieving my goal. I was leaving home soon. I was starting a new job, with new people, in a new environment. I wanted to bring Ana with me. I didn't want to be chasing her anymore. I have to admit that, in the back of my mind, I had a bit of concern about my health, but (and this is humiliating to admit) I was thinking, "Look, if those people in the holocaust could survive under the horrific conditions of starvation and hard labor, then my body surely can't be in any danger." Whether it was because I knew things were getting dangerous, or because I wanted to convince myself that I was "healthy," I decided to see my doctor. My blood pressure was 90/60. My heart rate was beating at fifty-five beats per minute. A few days later, my blood tests showed that I had anemia. Despite all of the pleadings from my mom, my dad, brothers, and sister to go into a hospital for treatment, I was determined to shut everything out to reach my goal. I was starting to control the binges a bit more because I would swallow almost an entire bottle of fiber pills before bed, or eat an entire bowl of wheat bran. To get those 4.75 pounds off, all I needed to achieve was a 17,000 calorie deficit over the next week or so. I thought I could pull it off in two or three weeks, although I wished it could be sooner. At this period in my struggle, I looked anorexic, but didn't officially have anorexia.

Unfortunately, I didn't "make weight" in the next 2-3 weeks because just as I lessened the frequency of the binges, they came roaring back. It's very difficult to explain, but when you have the urge to binge, it is irresistible. It is as if your brain produces certain chemicals that turn you into an animal that maniacally seeks food at any cost. It is almost as if you black out until the food is inside of you. Due to the binges, however, my weight was shifting from 125-133 pounds every week. I was abusing laxatives, enemas, and everything else to purge the extra calories. If this continued, Ana would say good-bye, my control would be gone, and I would be left alone and isolated. Most importantly, I would be a failure.

These binges were taking away my power and sense of control. My mom tried to explain that the binges were happening because I was starving myself. She supported me as I reluctantly went to doctors, psychologists, psychiatrists, and nutritionists. I did, however, have an idea. Most of the binges occurred around 2:00 or 3:00 a.m. when I would wake up in a ravenous state and consume anywhere between three to five thousand calories of food. I decided, therefore, that if I awoke during the middle of the night with the uncontrollable desire to binge, I would get up and walk around town for as long as I could. Yes, I would exercise in the middle of the night. That might stop these crazy urges. Unfortunately, while the idea was sound, I only did this once. I was just too exhausted to exercise under these conditions. So the binges continued. So did the daily starvation. I was comforted by the fact that you could still see all of my ribs and some of my veins. In fact, veins were bulging out from my stomach, protruding from the inside if my thighs, all the way down to my calves. While I was proud of this, though, there was still work to do.

Chapter Fifteen

Official Anorexia

Adversity Is Hard upon a Man

It wasn't time to get on the scale yet. I knew, and felt, that I was close to the necessary deficit and therefore near the 123.25 finish line. It was early June. At this point, I wasn't just exercising. I also took enemas and laxatives even when I didn't binge. Then, I started to write in my journal and note some additional foods and supplements that would help me reach my goal. My first entries included the following:

- Conjugated Linoleic Acid (CLA) because it prevents the body from absorbing fat;
- Apple Cider Vinegar (just drink it out of the bottle);
- 4 cups/daily of Green Tea (with cayenne pepper);
- Guarana (a stimulant);
- Drink excessive amounts of water, especially when eating anything;
- L-Tyrosine (regulated appetite and stimulates the central nervous system);
- L-Carnitine (helps regulate appetite and support healthy metabolism);
- Thyroid enhancers
- Fiber-rich foods; and
- Chromium (inconclusive but may aid in weight loss)

I was getting my hands on anything and everything possible. I could have tried some of those fat-burning fills like Hydroxy-Cut or Xantrax but I had used them over a year ago, and apart from making me feel jittery, they had no effect on me whatsoever. I didn't lose a single pound.

For the next week or so, I stuck to the plan. Some days things were so difficult that my body figuratively "died" on me. Truthfully, I had done all I could and there was nothing left to do except weigh myself. I had to wait until the next morning. You can't simply weigh yourself after exercise, because the lost fluid will give you a false reading. I had to suffer in silence. The moment had arrived. Everything I worked for was on the line. I desperately wanted anorexia. She was a person to me. She was my identity. She was my best friend. I was no longer Adam. I was Adam with the eating disorder. I needed that ultimate source of control. Anorexia reversed all the pain I had ever felt and turned it into power.

The next morning was hell. The scale was waiting for me. I walked into Bally's and went into the men's locker room. I walked toward the scale. It looked intimidating. The scale just had this potent presence that said to me, *Adam, it's not going to happen, so be prepared.* I wasn't prepared at all. I had no backup plan. This reading was going to determine my mood, my identity, my self-esteem, and whether there was something in the world that I had to live for.

The scale had been set at 150 pounds from the previous user, so I slowly began to inch it downwards, hoping that the time would not come when the metal bar evened out, indicating the positive determination of my weight. I was petrified as I moved it further and further down. I wouldn't look at the numbers because I was too frightened. The scale evened out and my weight was recorded. I looked at the number: 123 pounds!! 0.25 under what I needed to achieve! I had done it!! I was now a member of the exclusive club! I no longer had a bullshit, minor-league "eating disorder." Now I officially had anorexia. I was so thrilled and excited. It was over. Victory was mine. I was the champion of my body. I was skin and bones. I looked pale and sick. I fucking loved it. I had taken control of something by myself with no help whatsoever and turned it into a masterpiece. I was no longer a worthless human being. I had power. I had control. Anorexia was my best friend, and no one, and I mean no one, was going to take her away from me. She was the greatest gift I ever received and the best and most supportive friend that I had because, in my most vulnerable and uncontrollable moments, she gave me what I needed most: respect, control, love, self-acceptance, self-respect, and a feeling that I could conquer anything regardless of what people thought. Ana gave me freedom. She gave me liberation. After all, I had done it. After all of the downturns in my life, I had accomplished an incredible goal. It was just like those people who climb to the top of Mount Everest, go through hell to get there, but somehow, through sheer will and determination, make it to the top, where the feelings of victory, euphoria, and accomplishment abound. This was the day for joy and celebration.

That never happened. When I hit the 123 pound mark and in the days following, there was no one to celebrate with me. In fact, it was the opposite. My mom, who for the last few months had witnessed my obsession with weight loss, tried to get it into my head that I was abnormally irrational. My dad, brother, and sister came to my apartment and, as hard as they tried to conceal it, I could see the shocked looks on their faces when they saw me. I was Adam with anorexia. Everybody knew it. To them, celebration was the last thing on their mind; fear and worry were penetrating my apartment. I had worked out like a madman to get from 226 to 123 pounds, but no one seemed to care. They were actually telling me that I desperately needed to gain weight. They were wrong. Fuck them. I was a different person now. I could not be controlled or influenced. I had the power.

Unbelievably, though, when I reached my goal, something happened that tested the outer limits of my sanity. As quickly as the euphoria, control, and self-respect came from reaching 123, so too did the depression, insecurity, lack of self-esteem, and self-hatred. In other words, my world and the real world suddenly merged. It was anorexia's version of the cocaine crash. I was in disbelief. Oh my God. Ana was supposed to erase this. The victory that I achieved from anorexia wasn't what I thought it would be. It was accompanied by isolation, loneliness, disappointment, and meaninglessness. I couldn't understand why. I couldn't understand why it had happened so quickly. I felt the same betrayal as I had when Amy got pregnant. The finish line was actually a re-introduction to all of the feelings, emotions and memories that I tried to suppress. It was a realization that everything that I did in the old world, whether it was the people-pleasing Adam, the fake Adam, or the depressed Adam, was still a part of me that I had to come to terms with. I didn't want to admit this, but my mind was forcing me to, just as the binges were forcing me to eat.

In other words, the issues that I'd had before Ana remained the same after I reached the official point of anorexia. Ana was a temporary fix, a shield from my problems. It could not, however, erase the issues from my past that I needed to confront. She protected me from dealing with those issues because I was not capable of addressing them at that time. Yet, contrary to what I thought, I could not permanently escape them. I could keep Ana alive and stay at 123, or even go lower. But no matter how small I got, I could not minimize the severity of my depression, lack of self-esteem, feelings of inadequacy, and self-loathing. That was the hardest thing for me to realize. It wasn't supposed to be this way. Ana was supposed to save me from my life. Instead, she brought me right back to the old world. I didn't have a way out. If I had to go back to the other world and confront those issues, would I have to leave anorexia behind? What could life possibly be without Ana?

Ironically, a day or two after I reached 123 pounds, I went on a horrific binge. Ice cream, peanut butter, candy bars, Reese's, Snickers, ham and egg sandwiches, and Dunkin' Donuts. For the first time, though, I didn't freak out when I binged. I sat on my couch and went to sleep. When I woke up, I went back to Dunkin' Donuts and bought twelve donuts, most of which were chocolate frosted and Boston crème, more ham and cheese sandwiches, and ice cream. I ate all of that. Then I called my mom from my apartment and screamed at the top of my lungs. The scream had no words or discernible words in it. It was just the scream of a desperate man who was losing control over the only thing he ever had control of in his entire life. It was slipping away, and I didn't feel like I could do anything about it.

My mom didn't know what to say or do. I was in an emotional breakdown. I couldn't exercise because I was too fat to move. I just didn't feel like giving myself laxatives, enemas, or diet pills because, to be honest, I always knew it would purge only a small portion of the calories. I just kept going around in circles asking myself, *is Ana fighting me or is my body fighting Ana?* I guess it didn't really matter, because I was in for a difficult journey. I had a moment of clarity and honesty at this point. I would be in for a long journey of recovery and self-discovery. My emotional investment had failed.

I never saw 123.25 pounds again. Not for a day, not for an hour, not for a minute, not for a second. The closest I got was 127.8 pounds. After two years of eating foods that would make most people vomit, after two years of exercising like an Olympic athlete, I ultimately had only one day where I could claim that I suffered from anorexia. I met Ana, I experienced the euphoria, the accomplishment, the self-worth, the need to feel that I could accomplish even the most challenging things, and the sense that I was a human being worth living a happy life. But as soon as I felt those emotions, Ana let me go and she was gone forever. One day.

In that one day, I experienced the highest of highs, and the lowest of lows. My opinion of myself, my view of the world, my view of people, and my view of my immediate future; my belief in myself, my values, and my capabilities; and my ability to reach my dreams, express myself, feel in control of something, and be my authentic self with no apologies or regrets, changed. These were the gifts that made me, and continue to make me, thankful for my journey through anorexia. Little did I know that this was only half of the battle. Anorexia did not only exist to give me those things; it also existed to take them all away. I had to confront the real me without Ana. I had to address the traumatic experiences that occurred in my past and deal with the depression and disillusionment. I eventually did.

Chapter Sixteen

123 Pounds

Too Late to Realize My Mistake

I strongly believed that the positive qualities I developed — a sense of control, empowerment, and confidence — were the result of being able to reach anorexia. The problem was that I found them in the wrong, nearly deadly place. Also, anorexia really didn't give me these qualities. It was the opposite. It reinforced the difficult issues that I had never confronted. Ana controlled me. Ana weakened and took advantage of me. Ana was evidence of my addictive qualities. I was starving my body. I was a compulsive exerciser. I abused laxatives. I was a binge eater. I lived in isolation. I eliminated family and friends from my life. I said terrible things to my loved ones. I was not only the person I used to be in the other world, I was worse. As much as I hated to admit it, a new beginning was necessary.

As August of 2007 approached, I was about to begin my first semester as a law school professor. To say that I was nervous would be an understatement. I was scared. I had never taught before, I had never been to this city, I did not know a single person, and I had no idea where I was going to live. On top of this, I was still not eating normally, was hungry all of the time, and weighed 130 pounds. I drove to the city even though it took me over twenty hours. I wanted to be alone, settle into an apartment, and get to know the city. Unfortunately, that only lasted about a week. Then I told my mom to come visit me because I was too weak to find an apartment, furniture, or do much of anything else. I needed help. So she flew down and did everything for me. She also stayed longer to support me through the first couple of weeks I was teaching. Thanks, Mom.

I really didn't know if I was going to make it as a teacher. I was still teetering on the edge of a nervous breakdown. I was deathly afraid of speaking in front of a classroom full of students. I was afraid of making a fool of myself. I had failed at everything in my adult life and was filled with self-doubt. I was so nervous as my first day of teaching approached that I started binge-eating and compulsively exercising. I was an emotional wreck. My mom considered calling the school's Dean and saying that I just simply could not, in my physical condition, perform the job effectively. I had the courage, however, to move forward. I had to try. I had to see if I could accomplish something other than self-starvation. After all, teaching was one of my dreams, and the opportunity to live your dreams doesn't come along very often.

As the first day of school approached, I was introduced to my supervisor and some of the professors, which provided me with a measure of calm. I also saw the classroom where I would be teaching and met my teaching assistant. At the very least, I could now put faces to the names with whom I would be working. Unfortunately, I still did not know how I would react when thirty first-year students walked into my classroom staring at me as if I was some threatening authority figure. Would I freak out? Would I be so nervous that I would make a fool of myself? Would people laugh at me? What was going to happen? I just had no idea and would only find out when the moment arrived.

My first class was scheduled at 9:00 on a Tuesday morning. I decided to go to the classroom at 8:40 a.m. to organize my papers and the syllabus and just to get a general feel for being in the classroom, at the podium, and looking out at the students. It was scary. Then, I had a sudden panic attack and started sweating profusely. So I immediately went to the restroom, washed my face, and looked in the mirror. I said, "Adam, you can do this. Give this your best shot and you will be fine." I had never before engaged in this type of self-talk, but when I entered the classroom and it was full, I felt more in control of the situation. I was nervous when I first started talking; my voice cracked a bit and my breathing became shallow. Well, that lasted for about fifteen seconds when I broke the ice with a joke, saying, "Ok, listen, I've met a lot of the professors here and every one of them thinks I am a student that looks about twenty years old (which I did). Well, let me tell you, I am actually thirty-one years old, and I swear that I know how to teach this course." They smiled, which made me feel more comfortable. Much to my surprise, the class went well. My first day was over! I did it! I went back to my mom's hotel room and we were ecstatic! At that point, I knew, and I say this not in hindsight but from foresight, that my teaching career was going to be a good one. For the first time in a long time, I had accomplished something that I found meaningful.

I was now living with a passion, with an energy that reflected a sense of purpose and meaning. What I envisioned on the inside was now reflected in reality and, for the first time in years, I felt a sense of true happiness. It happened so fast. The sudden realization about my eating disorder was shocking. I still couldn't eat properly, I still binge ate, and the scale still controlled me, but I felt respected. Most importantly, I felt that I could make a difference in the world. Throughout my teaching career, I truly believe that I accomplished that to a degree. I helped inspire my students to live and fight for their passions. I taught them never to conform, or settle for less than what they truly wanted in life. I shared my story with them, so that they could learn from my mistakes and be empowered to live life their own way and on their own terms. I developed friendships that would last a lifetime.

I spent four years teaching a wonderful group of law students who are good people, good lawyers, and, now, good friends. I am also proud of my teaching style, which is unconventional. I never took "roll call" in my class, I had no "attendance" policy, and in all respects I treated my students like adults. They responded in kind, by producing professional quality work and by dedicating themselves to performing well in my class. I always cared about and genuinely loved my students. I drafted so many recommendations that I cannot even count them, served as a reference for all of my students, and was delighted to hear how successful they were after law school. That, to me, is the essence of what makes a good teacher. I had the time of my life teaching, meeting such wonderful people, and being a part of a special city that is like no other.

When I first started teaching in 2007, I knew that I would never get back to Ana (123.25), and that was ok with me. I was 130 pounds and significantly underweight, but wasn't ready for a full recovery just yet. I didn't need 123.25, but I still needed to be "sick." I still needed the eating disorder label. That, though, was the essence of the problem. If you're not willing to make any attempt at recovery, you will always be stuck in some "in-between" struggle with food, weight, and body image. That's where I was. If I could not bring myself towards recovery from Ana, I would still be anorexic even if I couldn't have anorexia.

The reason for my reluctance was very simple. I still didn't want to admit that my eating disorder was "bad" for me. I still wanted to believe that it had taken care of me in my darkest days and provided me with the kind of self-validation that I had never experienced in my life. I wanted to believe that it was my "friend" because I had made it so much a part of me and it helped me through the most difficult time in my life. If I attempted any "recovery," I felt like I would be betraying the only thing that ever made me truly happy and I could not deal with that. I felt like I knew more than everyone else. Even if they thought my eating disorder was threatening my health, they didn't know that it was my life before anorexia that had actually been poisonous to my well being. How could I turn away from my best friend? The answer when I started teaching, and for the next couple of years, was that I couldn't. I couldn't break up with Ana.

That's what started the Ten-Mile Morning. Every day, before teaching, binge or no binge, I made sure to run ten miles. I knew that this exercise would help control my weight and keep me within striking distance of Ana. I called it the ten-mile morning because every time I opened my eyes in the morning, it was like an automatic ritual: get my shorts and shirt on, put on my sneakers, and run ten miles which, for me, took almost two hours. Some days if I thought ten miles wasn't enough, I'd add a few more at the end of the day. The ten-mile morning represented my insurance against weight gain, against failure, and against losing everything for which I had struggled over the past year. I didn't want to become fat and let it all become just a memory. I was a good teacher with an eating disorder, and those were the facts. I was as faithful as ever to anorexia. My days, my mood, my ability to function, were based upon my ability to burn those calories in the morning and create such a negative caloric deficit that I would have to overeat tremendously to even risk gaining a quarter of a pound. I ran the same route every day. At every point, I made sure that those ten miles were my "alarm clock," my fierce defender against the 226-pound monster that I had been.

Ultimately, though, while I was feeling validated on the outside, there simultaneously festered within me the same feelings of depression, low self-esteem, anger, sorrow, and inner pain. It was a complete paradox of emotions. Yet what would life possibly look like if I gave up my eating disorder? I would be living in the eternal sunshine of a spotless mind. It would be as if the world was a blank slate to me. I would be born again. What things would I like? What places would I want to go to? What type of people would I gravitate toward? Who would I be? Would I be liked, hated, or treated with indifference? Ten-mile morning allowed me to evade answering these existential questions. It also did more than that. It demonstrated the living war and conflict that waged inside of me. I was a genuine person, but I was hiding many secrets. Yet my running was real. My ten-mile morning was real. My eating disorder was real. It had certain realities that contained grains of truth and, no matter how destructive, they seemed constructive and cathartic to me. Truth meant everything to me. My running gave me truth. My restricting gave me truth. Everything else seemed false.

Ten-mile morning was also directly connected to my eating habits. It wasn't just ten-mile running, it was ten-mile eating. I brought my starvation regimen from home with me to my new city. Unfortunately, along with it came the binges. The next year-and-a-half was an awful binge-purge cycle. I had my ten-mile mornings, sometimes seventeen-mile days, and binged about three to four times per week. As much as I tried to restrict my food intake, absolutely nothing, and I mean nothing, worked. Literally, about every other day, I found myself binging, purging through excessive exercise, and then starving my body. I would sometimes run to complete exhaustion. I started doing my Bikram Yoga classes again. Burning calories was as important as teaching. What I needed most, after all of the binging and purging, was to step on the scale and assess the damage. I so desperately wanted to be just a few pounds away from 123.25. As much as I had convinced myself that I didn't need to be at a certain weight, the fact was that I needed to feel that I could go back to Ana quickly if I so desired. Unfortunately, because of the binging, I had refused to weigh myself for fear of what the scale might say. Now, I just felt compelled to do it, to face my God. The scale's reading: 145 pounds. It felt like the death of a loved one. Ana had broken up with me, and there wasn't a single thing that I could do about it, or maybe I could.

Whether it was the binging, starving, compulsive exercise, or reliance on the scale, one thing that I had to admit, and was almost ready to admit, was that I was now helpless against anorexia. I was a living contradiction. I was an intelligent person, but lacking the most basic common sense in elementary areas, such as food and nutrition. I thought I was in control, but I was being controlled. As the days and months went by, I knew that I couldn't beat it alone. I needed professional help, but I still wasn't ready to give up the disorder. So I made a compromise. I would get help but secretly try to keep Ana alive to some extent. I wasn't about to completely abandon everything that had meant so much to me for the past several years, even though I knew that it could destroy me.

Chapter Seventeen

The Beginning of the Recovery

Going Our Separate Ways

I started to become suspicious of anorexia. The suffering that I had endured, whether it be the fiber pills, laxatives, binges, purges, physical complications, or emotional breakdowns, made me think that maybe, just maybe, I needed to find a way out. I felt dejected and alone. Was this eating disorder a logical extension of my personality and thus an inescapable fate to which I was forever sentenced? Could I really have been this wrong about my best friend for this long? I simultaneously hoped not and hoped so. I knew that my self-denial had to end. So, after nearly two years of teaching, I made the ultimate decision to seek help. I didn't know what to expect.

I sought help because, while thinking doesn't always change, feelings do. I was tired of all of the inner conflicts and contradictions. The writing was on the wall, and I couldn't ignore it anymore — I was losing the battle. The feelings of low self-esteem, self-hate, and inadequacy remained. Everything that was good was slowly going back to being bad. I had to accept this realization, even though it made me cry.

In other words, maybe it really wasn't food itself that was the issue. Maybe it had to do with some of the things that happened earlier in my life which left me with those feelings of low self-esteem and disgust towards myself. I started to understand that anorexia involved so much more than just food and weight. It involved control and bringing something to my life that had meaning and purpose. Despite everything that anorexia gave me, I still had to confront my inner feelings and deal with the emotional traumas that I had suffered in my life. Anorexia was such a contradiction: it made me feel powerful when, in fact, it was taking away all my power. Anorexia made me feel in control when, in reality, the control was being stripped from the very essence of my being. It made me feel that I was getting revenge on those who hurt me, but, in the end, I was only hurting myself, and those feelings of hate towards other people and myself were exactly what I needed to keep the disease alive.

The question that remains, though, is how can you escape and extricate yourself from the daily restricting, the over-exercise, the war with food, and the need to lose more and more weight? There is no simple answer. The fight with anorexia is an individual one, and nobody goes through the experience the same way. We all have different abuses and traumas that we've experienced, be they sexual, emotional, or physical, such as rape, rejection, the loss of a loved one, major medical issues, divorce at a young age, incest, molestation, and many other things. We have all travelled down different paths that led us to self-starvation. You don't simply get generic treatment for these problems. The treatment you need has to be your treatment. It has to fit with you. It is the first step in gaining control back in a life of which you have lost all control. It will be a very difficult decision and a very uncertain period in your life. But it's also one of the greatest gifts that you can give to yourself. Treatment reflects an unconditional love towards yourself and a commitment to take your life back and live it on your own terms.

While the future may be uncertain, uncertainty can be a beautiful thing because it leads to hope. Maybe, just maybe, there is a better tomorrow waiting on the other end of the road. I didn't know what to expect when it came to my battle with anorexia. Honestly, I was shocked when I reached 123 pounds and suddenly realized that all of my problems reappeared instead of disappeared. I knew that I was in for a fierce battle, but I didn't know whether I would win. I didn't know if I would just continue the ten-mile morning, the binge-eating, or, if things got bad enough, commit suicide. The idea of suicide was never far from my mind during these dark days, especially when the heavy binge-run cycle turned into high gear. I got so tired of losing control and then trying to regain it. I got so tired of eating 5,000 calories, running ten miles, and then starving myself. I had to do it so many times that I thought suicide might be a better exit out of this hell. For my sake, for the sake of my friends and family, I could no longer be just a professor of law. I had to be in treatment for anorexia nervosa.

My first step towards treatment was to start a journal. I wrote everything and anything that entered my mind. It reflected my experiences, my feelings, my fears, and my doubts. The idea of writing in a journal was not something I planned, but something that came naturally to me as a way to get out and express all of my inner feelings rather than let them stay inside and eat away at me. It was incredibly cathartic, because when I expressed my feelings it allowed me to reveal my most private and intimate thoughts in an assertive and truthful way.

Indeed, my journal was the first path to self-love and self-acceptance. It was a journey towards honesty. It was about accepting my strengths and weaknesses. It was about forgiving both myself and the others who had hurt me. My journal entries became the first step away from Ana. During some days I would take long walks in a park or meditate, and reflect on my thoughts, my pain, and my purpose. Some of my journal entries were meant to give me healthy control and reject old ways of negative thinking. I frequently go back to many of my entries for self-affirmation and positive self-talk, several of which I will share with you:

> I will live myself and my values. I will live happily, with purpose, meaning and compassion. I will listen to my body and intuition on physical, spiritual, and emotional levels. I will eliminate toxic people, places, and situations. I will embrace my whole self. I will embrace fear and love uncertainty because it means possibility. Think positively and believe in the power of positive thinking. Create your own reality through belief, action, and goals. Be proud of yourself, love yourself, and assert yourself.
>
> Develop your own individualized commandments for happy, healthy living, as well as balance, moderation, inner peace, harmony, and tranquility.
>
> Reward yourself with creative pursuits. Be kind to yourself. Nourish yourself. Comfort yourself. Forgive yourself. Love yourself. Take care of yourself. Be gentle with yourself and your body. Never deprive yourself.
>
> Do not conform. Think outside of the box. Feel the need to be understood. Be proud of yourself and love and be loved unconditionally. Do not depend on external things for happiness. Be sincere and honest. Originality is love.
>
> Food is not the enemy.
>
> Express and assert yourself. Love your body no matter what the scale says.
>
> It is ok to make mistakes as long as you did your best. Never compare yourself to or listen to other people who think they know better than you.
>
> Put yourself first. Be open to positive change. Let nature speak to you
>
> Acknowledge, instead of trying to avoid, your prior traumatic experiences. They are gifts upon which you can learn about yourself and grow. Use these experiences as positive tools and be humbled.

Then, near the end of 2007, I took the next step: I sought professional help. When I made the decision to seek treatment, it was as if the treatment was waiting for me. My first step was to look on the internet for psychiatrists, and I discovered one that lived near my apartment. So I scheduled an appointment. It turned out, miraculously, that my doctor specialized, among other things, in the treatment of people with eating disorders. I was happy because when a doctor specializes in what you are dealing with, you don't have to go through all of the background shit of how you got the disorder, why you restrict your food intake, and all the other issues underlying the problem.

He knew the disorder as well as anorexics or bulimics do themselves. We talked for about a half hour discussing where I was from, why I was here, and the symptoms and experiences that I was having. I told him, in the short time we had together, that I had been suffering from an eating disorder for the past two years and had lost 103 pounds while adhering to a "negative calorie" diet full of raw vegetables and veggie burgers. I explained the intensity of the exercise, from running, to yoga, to weight training, and expressed my utter lack of control over binge eating, which he quickly noted was my body's natural response to the food deprivation. I really liked this doctor because he genuinely cared about me, my condition, and about helping me get in a better position to enjoy my life. After I was done speaking, he began to tell me that I displayed all of the signs of an eating disorder and needed immediate treatment for my problem. He also diagnosed what is commonly called a co-morbid condition, because, along with the eating disorder, I also suffered from depression. Based on the information I gave him, he started me on Prozac, which he said would help with my depression and binge eating urges.

What was most important to my doctor was for me to see a team of therapists with whom he worked, because they specialized in treating people with eating disorders. He explained to me that I had to start seeing a social worker and nutritionist to work through the emotional and food-related issues that lay at the heart of anorexia. I was quite apprehensive but made the financial commitment because, at this stage, after all this time, I finally wanted to get better. To some degree, I still wanted to keep my eating disorder, but I knew that I couldn't. I was both optimistic and sad at the same time. I had to move forward, but I still yearned to go back.

I scheduled an appointment to see my therapist, Elizabeth Varino. She had an extraordinary amount of experience in treating people with eating disorders. When I walked into her office, she was welcoming, gentle, generous, and kind. It was obvious that she was there to listen and genuinely help me. I was shy at first. I didn't want to tell her about the bad things that I had done to my body for the purpose of trying to lose weight. I didn't want to tell her about the diuretics, enemas, or laxatives. I didn't want to tell her about the affairs, the drugs, or hookers. I didn't want to tell her about the ten-mile morning. Most of all, I didn't want to tell her about the emotional issues that were driving my eating disorder. I just felt embarrassed. However, as I talked to her, she shared some of her past traumas with me. I knew that she was someone I could trust, confide in, and feel comfortable with. She was real and I knew that she was going to be a vital part of my recovery. She was — and is — a wonderful person, a fantastic therapist, and someone that made me feel something that I never felt before: self-acceptance and self-respect.

As time went by and the trust between us built, I started to tell her about the extreme traumas that affected my life. I told her how inherently sensitive I felt as a young child and that, as far back as I could remember, I always experienced terribly low self-esteem. I told her how, as a child and continuing into adulthood, even the slightest criticisms would cause feelings of shame and self-hatred. I told her that, as a result of these feelings, I became a people pleaser by putting on a fake image of myself that everyone would like. I did anything and everything to gain the approval of others. The only way for me to feel any semblance of happiness was for me to get positive compliments from others, because I had no love or acceptance of myself. She didn't just listen to me — she heard me. She "got it." I could tell that she had been to the same places in her life and that she was truly compassionate and understanding.

I was deeply angry at myself. I told her how much emotional pain and depression I had felt in my life, how not knowing the answer to or source of this pain had left me suicidal. I told her how I had used alcohol, drugs, hookers, and anything else to escape the pain. I told her that I'd had two affairs with married women and I was ashamed for both. I told her how awful I felt for snorting cocaine, smoking crack, and stealing money from my dad to fuel my habit. I told her how much I regretted the awful things I'd said to my family. I told her how angry I was at the people with whom I worked, as well as the girlfriends that I used to date, who always took advantage of me because I didn't have the ability to exercise my voice or draw boundaries. Most importantly, I told her that I was sorry to be me. I hated myself, and the events in my life only confirmed that I was right to hate myself. Perhaps most importantly, I told her that anorexia was the one thing that gave me power, self-esteem, and a sense of control. Now that I was getting treatment, I told her, I was petrified. I didn't know what was going to happen next. I didn't want to go back to the pre-anorexic days, and I didn't know what a post-anorexic world would look like. When I said these things to her, I was afraid that she might "look down" on me and lose respect for me. After all, I had done some terrible things that hurt other people and if she felt even the slightest anger towards me, then therapy would have to end.

It was the opposite. She was understanding and empathetic. It made me feel so wonderful, as if I was lifting a thousand pounds of pressure off my back, to have a person to listen who truly understood my pain. While I was embarrassed to say these things, it was so cathartic. I needed to discuss my past in order to reach the core origins of anorexia. As a 33-year-old man, I still had no voice; my opinion was still not respected and my feelings of self-hatred and lack of self-esteem never left me. It hurt to talk about these bad memories. I wanted to pretend that they never happened, but that is exactly why eating disorders develop: you have not confronted and dealt with difficult emotional feelings and past traumas that lie at the heart of your pain.

Elizabeth helped me come to terms with why I had made those choices during my life. She told me something that changed my feelings of self-hate — that the behaviors I engaged in weren't my fault. I wasn't a bad, immoral, or shameful person for doing the things that I did. There could be nothing further from the truth. What Elizabeth helped me understand, in the more than two years of therapy which continues to this day, is that I messed with hookers, did cocaine, and had sex with a much older woman because I was trying to "numb" myself out of my own reality, with which I could not cope. As she explained, that was not surprising because, as a young man with feelings of inadequacy, insecurity, and low self-esteem, I did not have the tools to cope with the various traumas that affected my life. So the natural response was to seek out other ways to "avoid" and "escape the reality" that I did not want to face. I needed to escape from the "people pleaser," the fake person, the person whose mental health depended on other people, the self-hating loser, and the worthless me, the one who was undeserving of loving or capable of being loved. The alcohol, drugs and hookers were my coping mechanism because I had no others.

Elizabeth helped me in such critical ways. She helped me to understand exactly why I'd acted in these destructive ways and how these behaviors were almost the logical result of, and natural response to, the world that I was experiencing. In other words, I wasn't doing anything wrong; I was doing everything right because I was trying to take care of myself in the best way possible. My actions had nothing to do with judgment or moral transgression. This insight began our work down the difficult road of stopping the self-hatred, the self-loathing, and the self-destruction. She continued to provide me with plausible and believable explanations connecting my behaviors to specific emotional traumas that I suffered, such that I could literally trace them to my destructive actions throughout my life. In other words, there was a pattern, or roadmap, to my conduct. All of my addictions and conduct were in response to life events that fueled the negative feelings about myself, particularly the belief that I had no control or power in my life.

The trust that developed between Elizabeth and me only grew as I revealed more and more of the intimate details of my life. I was always so worried about what people thought of me. I had this inherent need to please everyone around me, even those that I despised or would never associate with. I wanted to tell so many people to fuck off. But I couldn't. I was afraid. I lived in fear of being attacked. Not physically, but emotionally. I had no ability to fight back, and when there were clear instances when I could have — and should have — I ran away. I gave my power to everyone else. If you wanted to make fun of me for something I didn't do, fine. If you wanted to blame me for something I did do, fine. If you wanted to make fun of something I had no involvement in, fine. I would just walk away, hating myself. The core problem here, as Elizabeth explained, was that I governed all of my conduct by an overarching moral principle. I viewed everything in terms of black or white. I viewed my behavior as "good" or "bad," "shameful," or "disgraceful," and when I heard those terms, I began to define myself according to a moral framework. And whenever things went "wrong," I always felt that they were "my fault" and that I was a "bad person." Those were precisely the types of feelings that led to low self-esteem, feelings of worthlessness, and thoughts of suicide. It was beginning to all make sense — it was never about morality — it was about me and my ability to overcome the past so that I could live happily in the present.

That was only the beginning. Now that I knew this about myself, I had to start working to change my actions towards myself and other people. I had to learn healthy coping skills. I had to learn important life lessons. Of course, knowing what you have to do is far different than feeling that you have the strength to change. This is particularly true when certain behaviors, like those associated with eating disorders, have governed your life for an extended period. In fact, even after these revelations, I couldn't put Elizabeth's words into action. I needed some control so badly, and I didn't know anywhere else to get it than from my old best friend. So I kept exercising daily at a relentless pace. Yes, the ten-mile morning continued even though I was so exhausted. If I binged, it became the fifteen to seventeen-mile day. Despite my knowledge, my actions weren't changing. As Elvis said, "Reason can't stand in for feeling."

For Elizabeth and me, our work turned to focusing on my patterns of thinking and belief systems. I had lived for many, many years in a pattern of negative thinking. I would say things to myself like, "Adam, you're a fucking idiot," and "you're so stupid." This ultimately contributes to feelings of inadequacy and a lack of self-esteem. It also leads to negative conduct, such as alcohol and drug abuse, which, I might add, does not suddenly disappear because your therapist provides a detailed roadmap of the reasons why it was not your fault and why you were just handling the situation as best as you could. You don't automatically begin to love yourself unconditionally and achieve self-acceptance. It takes time because you still have to confront the specific traumatic events that affected your life, come to terms with them, forgive yourself and others (if required), and then leave them in the past. You also need to engage in the type of introspection where you see yourself as that innocent child, with uncompromising hopes and dreams. You have to understand that you can live a passionate, meaningful, and fulfilling life. Lost dreams are never really lost. You can get them back. Hope may be dangerous, but it is also an essential part of the truth that change is possible in every one of us. This is the only way to move forward.

I initially met with Elizabeth twice a week. We talked about the disconnect, or new connection, between my feelings and behaviors. It took us a long time to deconstruct all of the events in my life that had caused me so much pain. Through all of it, there was one truth that remained the common denominator: I experienced emotional traumas, and I should not blame myself for my actions. The affair when I was seventeen was not my fault. I was a sensitive person and wanted to be loved by someone other than my family. I wasn't successful at those law firms because I was a bad lawyer. It was because the practice of law was not for me; it wasn't what I thought it would be, and I wanted to work in a profession that, for me, felt more meaningful and fulfilling. It was not my fault for having a second affair. I was a very unhappy lawyer during that time, looking for love and affection anywhere I could find it. Also, I truly did love her and did the best I could to make her happy. I should not be ashamed for doing drugs or messing around with hookers. This was the only coping mechanism that I had to escape from a horrible inner and outer reality that was so far removed from my dreams.

Furthermore, I shouldn't hate myself for hating myself because I had done nothing wrong to think of myself that way. In fact, I was a good, honest, and loving person. I shouldn't hate myself for developing anorexia, or recovering from it. I was just looking for some control in a world that had caused me to suffer a nervous breakdown. It was now time for me to be kind to myself, to learn how to love myself, and to engage in the type of self-acceptance that would liberate me from the chains that I had placed around my existence. Elizabeth's insights not only allowed me to have a more balanced view of the situation, but they helped me to stop the self-hate and start the process of self-healing. It was time to discover my true self and to find all of those things about me that I never knew existed. The journey would be a special one, where I would be reintroduced to myself.

As a result of confronting these traumas, my feelings about myself slowly began to change. Moreover, because they are inextricably linked, my behaviors began to change. I stopped the negative thought patterns and made every effort to stop saying things like, "you are worthless," "you are a loser," and "you are stupid." Instead, I used tools that Elizabeth taught me, called "positive self-talk" and "daily affirmations" (sentences that assist you in having a positive daily outlook). This completely changed my way of thinking. Rather than the old criticisms, I would now, on a daily basis, say things to myself like, "you are a good person and entitled to be happy," "you love yourself and deserve to be loved just the way you are," "you are doing the best that you can and that will always be good enough," "you are entitled to pursue your passions in life," and "you deserve to eat and nourish your body." Saying these things felt awkward at first, but slowly these thoughts begin to transform themselves into feelings. You begin to feel positive about yourself and believe that you are indeed worthy of love, self-respect, and self-acceptance. After all, everyone is entitled to a life filled with these feelings.

Anorexia simply cannot exist in this state of mind. Just as the negative self-talk affirmed my self-hatred, the ongoing positive self-talk was starting to let me feel good about myself and happy with the person I was at that moment. I wasn't looking back at the past or toward the future. I was just living at peace in the moment and my mind was undergoing a fundamental change. If I did not want to engage in "positive self-talk" on a particular day, I could always write my feelings down in a journal, which allowed me to express myself, rather than keep my emotions festering inside. This, combined with seeing Elizabeth twice a week, allowed me to have healthy ways of communicating my thoughts and emotions, which is essential not only for people with eating disorders, but for anyone who seeks a healthy relationship with themselves and others. Over time, positive self-talk and journaling became my first "healthy" coping mechanisms and the gateway towards resuming some semblance of normal eating habits. There were certainly bad days where I starved myself and ran seventeen miles, but I had finally built a foundation for recovery, something I could hold on to with the hope that things would get better.

Of course, I still had to live in the "real world." As soon as I left Elizabeth's office, I had the venture back to a world filled with materialism, envy, gossip, and opportunism. I simply could not rely on my twice-a-week sessions with Elizabeth, and these daily affirmations, to obviate the negative energy that came my way during the rest of the week, which sometimes triggered the ten-mile mornings, the starvation, and the self-loathing. What was I going to do? The positive self-talk and daily affirmations helped, but they were only part of a larger strategy that I hoped would soon take down this disorder. I still had my problems. I was still disempowered and had difficulties drawing boundaries, asserting myself, or using my voice. I didn't have that many healthy areas of control. I still struggled with past memories and self-doubt. However, I would consistently review past and present entries in my journal, which, along with the life lessons that I'd learned, were amazingly cathartic. Just as I shared with you before, here are some additional entries that helped me during those difficult days:

> Adam, you are entitled to happiness; you are deserving of happiness and good days, you are deserving of pleasure. Yes, some days will be bad and some expectations and hopes not met, but you are entitled to and worthy of what you want. Your happiness is all that matters. Ask yourself, what do I want in each moment and know that you are worthy of and entitled to and deserving of it. You are a good person, Adam.

The journey of self-discovery, the power to see new things, to experience new things, to open yourself up to change, is a lifetime journey with limitless possibility. Embrace that infinite possibility, the limitless, but always respect your limitations. This is critical to balance, moderation, mindfulness, and self-awareness. Do not fear the unfamiliar. Embrace the potential for discovery that lies within it.

Love the stillness of nature and its permanence.

This is about a lifetime of love, not a daily struggle. Self-love is the key to self-sustainment in the face of hardship and surprise. Remember, the bad days, or slip-ups, are not failures of the self, they are humble reminders of the demon's power and your need to be respectful of and humbled by that power as you [begin to] plan, manage, develop, and discover yourself, inner peace, and the environment, routine, and surrounding that allow for you to experience mind/body integration with nature on its truest, yet most powerful level.

Give yourself credit/be proud of yourself for the daily choices that reaffirm your individual values, purpose, and unique desires ... don't be too hard on yourself.

Mindfulness is critical to self control/balance. Self-awareness is the key to healthy integration, and Inside Out Expression.

Nature, yoga, mediation — existing in silence — ...is the path to inner sanctuary and peace. It is the foundation of breakthroughs and insights about me and my connection to the physical self and world around me.

Learn to relax and give yourself a break. Be less self-critical. Learn to be comfortable thinking of nothing and just living/feeling in the moment ... always be positive/life affirming...keep a positive perspective [and]...respect your uniqueness.

Embrace the concept of transcendence of me, into a stronger self, integrated with nature, simplicity, truth, beauty and humbled by the earth and all of the vastness and beauty. I love the limitlessness of life and the limitations as well. I love merging of the opposites.

Everything is part of the good. There is no negative emotion, everything is part of the good and integrated into the positive and life-affirming self.

When I integrate to the [outside] world, I will do so from the inside (self) – out. I am in control of my choices, of my moments, of my life, of my spirit, of my environment, of everything. I love life. I love Earth. I love Nature. I love simplicity. I love truth.

Listen to your body and Intuition. Trust yourself.

> Sometimes, despite everything you do, it [things] … just won't develop or turn out as expected. Don't panic or be defeated. This is ok … bad moments are impermanent disappointments that give you a great gift — the gift of a permanent lesson/principle from which to gain new perspective for the moment as well as all moments. It is a positive experience. There is no room for or acceptance of negative energy, through self-talk or perspective. In every moment, good or bad, concepts of disappointments are merely words, not states of being. Remember, in silence, in nothingness, there can be no negative emotions.
>
> Be proud of yourself and your daily moments and achievements … be still, silent and relaxed in stressful moments.
>
> You have invented and created your own coping mechanisms and this is the key to a stronger self and self-esteem.
>
> Always be accountable but not too hard on yourself.

I also realized how much I loved nature — walking through neighborhood parks, just admiring the stunning beauty of the trees, water, and animals. I discovered how much I enjoyed meditating and that feeling of silence and simplicity. In those moments, all negative energy was eliminated. The only thing I could hear was the sound of my breath, and through this process, I felt "centered" and "balanced" emotionally. I felt I was gaining a sense of control that was based on something real: a love for my authentic self. I also realized something else — there was no need to dislike others and have a negative view of the world. It did nothing but take me away from my recovery and waste my emotions on something that I could not control. I had to create my own positive and honest world. I had to learn to be and love myself. By doing that, I could not only live in the "real" world, but I could attract people who would love me unconditionally.

Indeed, the next and very important step in my recovery was to apply my new coping tools and use them in my interactions with others. The first thing I had to do, as alluded to above, was to start drawing boundaries with my family, friends, and romantic partners. I had to put myself first. The "people pleaser" had to vanish. I had to start making decisions based on what was healthy for me and not on what was beneficial to other people. I had to be kind to myself and learn to take care of myself in a loving way.

So that's what I started doing. For example, in my relationship with my Amy, I stopped taking her calls as frequently, and when I did talk to her, I limited the duration of our conversation. When I spoke with my wonderful parents, I told them that there was to be no discussion at all about my eating disorder or about my weight. I explained that I was in treatment with excellent people and that I would eventually recover and be healthy. So, during the Christmas holiday, nobody, not my sister, brothers, mom, dad, or family friends, even discussed the subject of weight, diets, or how I looked. That not only made me feel comfortable, but it validated me in the sense that my voice mattered and, by using it, I could achieve positive changes in my life.

Also, Elizabeth helped me to understand that when I did draw boundaries, I didn't necessarily have to give any explanation or reason for my decision. Sometimes, just saying "no" is enough. Engaging in this activity is called "using your voice," and it brought to me an overwhelming feeling of empowerment. Of course, when I did this, I often felt very guilty, because sometimes, by putting myself "first," I felt like I might be hurting or disappointing other people with whom I had personal or professional relationships. After all, this was the first time in my life where I was putting other people second. The reality, however, was that, for the first time, I wasn't letting people take advantage or exploit me, and that created an atmosphere around me that I finally didn't need to escape on a daily basis.

Chapter Eighteen

Fighting the Battle

We Can't Go On Together

Therapy is only half of the battle. Next is a more difficult step: the return to normal eating. It is so difficult because anorexia fucks with your body image. When I looked in the mirror, even when I was 125 pounds, I saw the reflection of an obese man. Anorexia was playing tricks with my mind, making me believe that I was fat when it was precisely the opposite. Instead of being my friend, it was starting to betray me and bring me back into its grasp. Those images in the mirror and the notion of "normal" eating implied one thing and one thing only: I was going to gain weight. The mortal sin for anorexics is weight gain. It is associated with failure, shame, and guilt. I was scared because all of the progress that Elizabeth and I had made might be reversed if I gained weight. I didn't want that to happen.

I was scared to death. That's when I met Corey Walsh, my nutritionist, whom I continue to see weekly. Like Elizabeth, I would not be where I am today without Corey. She has helped and supported me in so many ways, not just with the return to normal eating, but with making me feel that my life is worth living. Of course, things weren't always this way. I told her when we first met, "food is the enemy," and, for me, calories were the most frightening thing on this earth. I knew the calorie content of every type of food I purchased. I would never even dare to eat something without knowing the calorie content, because then I would risk gaining weight. In fact, I memorized the calorie content of nearly all of the food I bought. Corey's difficult job, therefore, was to take me to the world where people eat without knowing how many calories are in their food, without being concerned about body image, and without fear of gaining weight. All of these irrational fears, Corey explained, were the product of an eating disorder that was controlling me. She was right.

I didn't want to go back to normal eating. Yes, I was petrified of gaining weight. Truthfully, though, I knew I might gain some. I was significantly underweight, and when I returned to anything resembling normal eating, I would be eating more calories and thus maybe gain some weight. As Corey explained, if I did gain any weight, it was simply my body's way of telling me that it needs to restore me to a more healthy and natural size. What Corey also said, however, was that normal eating would not cause me to become anything close to overweight. I was just going to be healthier and, as a result, happier. I had to accept this fact before I started the recovery process. I did — reluctantly.

During our first few sessions, though, Corey assured me that she had no intention of making me gain weight. Her goal was to get me to the point where I would not fear gaining weight from eating a variety of foods that were satisfying to me. Surely, she presumed, raw vegetables, spicy sauces, and veggie burgers could not, and did not, satisfy me on a daily basis. It was Corey's hope that we could get to a place where I could eat all of the foods I wanted and eat them until I felt satisfied. In other words, she wanted me to become connected to my hunger and fullness signals. It's called intuitive eating, because your body will tell you when it is hungry and needs fuel and it will tell you when it is comfortably full. If we could do that, then there would be no need to count calories, or do the ten-mile morning, because my physical activity and food intake would be more balanced and I would not gain weight. She made logical sense, but my eating disorder was all about emotion. She needed to get to that before I could return to food.

Before we assessed food intake, however, I had to get weighed. The scale was just standing there in the back of the room, and it had this ominous presence, as if my weight was going to be much, much higher than I anticipated. As scared as I was, I stepped on the scale and got a reading of 138 — 14.75 pounds away from Ana. Now, the last time I weighed myself I was 145, so I was happy and disappointed at the same time. I was hoping for 130 or less, even though Corey said that, at 138, I was still underweight. I hated that term. To me, "underweight" meant that you're too skinny but not strong enough to have an eating disorder.

After the weigh-in, it was time to determine my level of physical activity so that we could calculate my daily caloric needs. My exercise regimen was the ten-mile morning. I then told Corey that if I felt I had overeaten or, much worse, had a binge eating episode, I would up my daily exercise regimen to about 15-17 miles per day. She was surprised at how intense my daily workouts were. I told her that every morning when I woke up I ran ten miles because it was designed to act as a sword and shield — it may help me lose weight or, at the very least, it would prevent me from gaining weight.

Corey naturally asked me about my eating habits during the day, and I told her that I had been basically eating the same foods for about three years but had made some slight changes since moving to the city. After I ran my ten miles, I would eat a protein bar before I taught my class. For lunch, I would eat another protein bar and, by late afternoon, a third protein bar. This amounted to about 800 calories. For dinner, I would go to a salad bar, put every type of raw vegetable in my salad and then buy veggie burgers. That was my eating plan every day. However, I did express my concern about having these horrible binge eating episodes where I would consume between 3,000 and 5,000 calories in one sitting. To me, these episodes represented more than just failure. I viewed them as representing a part of my being that could take control of me whenever it wanted, rendering me helpless. In essence, there were times when I was scared of myself.

Given my fears, we had a very difficult journey ahead of us. Corey is a wonderful, caring, bright, and fantastic person, and I felt comfortable with her. She first began by saying that I was nowhere near getting the calories that my body needed to function normally. Running ten miles per day, and in some cases more, required about 3,000 calories and I was consuming, at most, about 1,500. These substantial caloric deficits, she explained, and the lack of "fat" sources in my diet, caused my body's metabolism to slow down in response to perceived starvation and, thus, led to binge eating. The only way to prevent this was to eat more food during the day, particularly food that I would find satisfying, because that would make it far less likely that a binge would occur.

She then asked what I would binge on, and I told her it was always ice cream, peanut butter, and other sugary foods. Well, she said, don't you see the connection? Peanut butter is highly caloric and provides a substantial amount of fat as well as protein. Ice cream and sugary foods contain simple carbohydrates that are easily digestible and thus provide the body with the quick caloric nourishment that it requires. Therefore, there were specific, underlying reasons connecting the binges to my eating habits. It was not a mystery. If I followed a more normalized eating plan, with the necessary intake of calories, fat, protein, and carbohydrates, then the binges would stop. At this point, though, I didn't believe that. The binges had shaken my foundation so much that I was afraid to put more "normal" foods, that I hadn't enjoyed in years, in my mouth for fear that if I did that, then I would uncontrollably gorge on everything in sight. For example, if I ate a slice of pizza, I would eat the whole fucking thing.

Aside from that, I wasn't sure if Corey completely understood my weight-gain fear, even as irrational as it may have been. I used to weigh 226 pounds. I was so petrified of gaining weight that if I even put a teaspoon of ice cream in my mouth, I thought I would get fat. How could I even entertain the notion of eating "fat" and carbohydrates? They were evil. Any intake of foods with that crap would surely make me gain weight and look like a balloon. And the image in my mirror confirmed how fat I looked! No matter how many times my nutritionist told me that my thinking was distorted, I didn't believe it, because I "felt" fat. To me, consuming any type of "normal food" was like committing a crime for which severe punishment would be warranted. I would feel shame because I was not being a good anorexic, in that I could not resist food. Wait, I'm supposed to be in recovery, right?

Corey and I talked and talked. I really liked her because she respected me, my opinion, and the situation I found myself in. Like Elizabeth, she "got it," and knew all about the dynamics of eating disorders. As the session continued, she slowly began challenging the disordered beliefs that I had about my body and food. First, there existed the perception, and then there was the reality. As Corey said, I may "feel" fat but fat is not a "feeling," like anger, sadness, or happiness. It is a mechanism used by the disorder to keep you within its control. Also, there are feelings, and then there are facts. I was 5'8" and 138 pounds. The normal weight range for my height and weight was 145-157 pounds. I was ten pounds underweight. So was I really fat? No. That belief was irrational, distorted, and a product of my eating disorder. What about my belief that food was the enemy? Why did I believe food was the enemy? Because I thought it could lead to massive overeating and weight gain. That's not true, though, if you are mindful of your meals and make good choices about the foods you consume. None of my beliefs could withstand the force of reason.

Specifically, for a person to gain one pound, he or she would have to consume 3,500 more calories than his or her daily caloric allowance, and that allowance is based primarily upon age and activity level. Thus, if a normal person needs 2,200 calories to sustain his or her weight, he or she would have to consume 5,900 calories in a single day to gain a single pound. In fact, though, he or she would not gain that pound because 10% of the body's intake is used to digest the food. Thus, 590 calories would have to be used to compensate for this binge. That would bring the total caloric intake to 5310, and when you subtract that by 2,200 you get 3,110. So, after all that eating, not a single pound is gained. Most importantly, however, is the fact that I discussed earlier: eating disorders are not about food or weight. I had to remember this on my journey toward normal eating.

Corey's conversations in the early sessions helped me tremendously because she used undeniable facts that somewhat altered my way of thinking. Anorexics do not think in the rational terms that Corey was discussing with me. Numbers and facts mean nothing. Yet I was starting to believe them because they made intuitive sense. Maybe I wouldn't gain weight if I ate some other foods. After all, other foods might have the same caloric content as the food I was eating, so what was I afraid of? What if I started eating 2-300 hundred more calories a day? Would I gain weight? Maybe not. I was running ten miles a day. Surely, I deserved to eat more than raw vegetables, right? Wouldn't it be better to eat a bit more during the day so that I didn't binge and consume thousands of calories at night? And if I did gain weight simply by altering my food intake, maybe my body was sending me a message. Maybe it was my body's way of telling me that I was at an unhealthy weight and needed more nourishment to restore me to normalcy. Maybe my body, not anorexia, was my friend.

As I slowly started to change my thinking, Corey and Elizabeth helped me each week by stressing the importance of positive self-talk and daily affirmations. I didn't react negatively to this suggestion because it had been the catalyst in helping me to rediscover my voice and draw boundaries with people. For example, by saying, "I will nourish my body today," "I will succeed today," "I will not binge eat tonight," "I will not starve my body today," "I will not get fat by eating normally," and "I may feel fat, but I am not fat," your positive thoughts transform into positive action. Many of my daily affirmations came from, and still do come from, the internationally well-known self-help expert Louise Hay, who has, on her website, a daily, positive affirmation that you can repeat to yourself to uplift your spirit and feel good about yourself. You can find it at http://www.louisehay.com/affirmations/. Elizabeth and Corey were so very helpful in challenging the feelings and beliefs that had been formed by my eating disorder. Now, it didn't always work. I binged several more times, starved myself many more times, and frequently ran the ten-mile morning. But I was now in the recovery process and, at the very least, I was more committed to getting better. That commitment was the enemy of my eating disorder.

While seeing Elizabeth and Corey consistently, I also had sessions with my wonderful and caring psychiatrist. I told him of the progress that I was making. However, I told him that my depression was still an issue, that I was having mood swings, binge eating episodes, and tremendous difficulty sleeping. I even told him that, despite my progress, "sometimes, I feel that I would be better off dead." It was true. After hearing my thoughts and feelings, I was prescribed three more medications: Topomax (to help curb binge eating), Lamictal (to help stabilize my moods), and Seroquel (to cure my difficulty sleeping). I could not believe that I was now on four different medications, in significant dosages.

Was I that fucked up? Was my mind that distorted and irrational that it needed four chemicals to pull me out of my depression, suicidal ideations, and eating disorder? I had no idea, but when I looked back at what I had done to myself and my body, I decided to trust his judgment. After all, he was the doctor and I was sick. I filled the additional medications and took them as prescribed. I can tell you now, and without hesitation, that these medications have saved me in so many different ways. Without them, I don't know if I could have come this far along in the recovery process. I have a fantastic psychiatrist and am grateful in every way.

Then it was back to Elizabeth. I always looked forward to our sessions, because I could be completely honest and forthcoming without the fear that she would judge me. We usually talked about the normal things that happened since the last time that I'd seen her and how I'd used my new coping skills to handle situations that I'd encountered. Did I use my voice? Did I draw boundaries? Did I express my true self? Sometimes yes, sometimes no. That was no longer good enough. It was time to set boundaries on a more consistent basis, so that I could be my authentic self and garner respect from others. If other people did not like me for that, then fuck them. Elizabeth's advice was — and still is — so inspirational because of its truth. I have not only gained respect by drawing boundaries, but I have gained friendships. People like me for who I am, not for the image I present. It's funny — when you live truthfully and allow your weaknesses and insecurities to show, people like you more.

Now it was back to Corey. I liked Corey very much, but it was always difficult to discuss the exercise and food issue. She asked me first about my exercise routine and I told her that I was still, on many days, running the ten-mile morning. Also, I was still eating the same raw vegetables and veggie burgers. This was especially troublesome because of my extreme activity levels. Corey expressed concern about my body, especially my heart, and told me to see my medical doctor (the fourth aspect of the treatment team) to have a physical and full blood-work. So I scheduled a session with my doctor, which would take place approximately ten days later. I also had to discuss a very similar problem with Corey. Much to my dismay, I was still having uncontrollable binge eating episodes every other day. I had never before binged with this type of frequency, intensity, or sheer volume. I simply was not in control of my eating disorder anymore. Also, I felt that I was in danger, because every time I binged I could hear my heart racing, as if it was shocked by the sudden amount of calories that I just consumed. Was this going to be my life? Was I going to struggle with binge eating forever? That would definitely make me gain weight and then I would be fat again. But I couldn't lose to peanut butter and ice cream. If I did, I would kill myself.

Corey understood this and gave me important advice. As you cross the bridge toward normal eating, there will be strong currents beneath you, and sometimes you will fall off the bridge, but the purpose is to get right back on track and continue to walk across that bridge with courage and commitment. Corey said that she was going to help me through this, but that there would be slip-ups along the way, because my body would now be receiving foods that it had been deprived of for years. For example, if I ate that steak that I'd deprived myself of for four years, I might eat two instead of one. It was as if, when I finally ate something that tasted good, lights went on in my head and I had this uncontrollable desire to eat everything in sight. That's why I feared so much the return to normal eating. However, Corey assured me, this is temporary, and it would pass as my eating became normalized over time. It was a matter of trusting my body.

Second, the positive self-talk before every meal was vital to help prevent a binge. Affirmations such as, "I love myself and am nourishing my body, but it does not want all of those extra calories," were so helpful. Positive self-talk and affirmations can go to great lengths to achieve the goals of both eating normally and preventing terrible binges. Also, you need to place yourself in a position where you cannot binge. For example, you can have lunch before going into an important meeting, or eat before going back to work. The point is that you need a plan before ingesting "normal foods." These strategies allowed me to begin, on a sporadic basis and with cautious optimism, to enjoy the wonderful foods that I wanted to eat. I realized that when you listen to your body's signals of hunger and fullness, then the threat of weight gain becomes almost non-existent. Now, for some individuals whose hunger and fullness signals have been compromised by the devastating effects of anorexia, it is important to know that these signals will come back and you will be able to understand when you are hungry and when you are comfortably full. So Corey's advice was not only helpful, but it almost seemed achievable.

So what foods would I try to eat as we built our bridge to normal eating? I told Corey that I really liked peanut butter and jelly, most types of seafood, tofu, nuts, and fruits and vegetables. I was, and still am, a pescatarian, so that made things a bit harder. We started slow. Was there anything that I could eat for breakfast that I might enjoy? Well, I liked cereal and oatmeal, and sometimes eggs. What about lunch? I was comfortable having a salad, with tofu or salmon with it. I would put a variety of vegetables on the salad, and maybe walnuts or almonds to get my fat source. For dinner, she and I agreed that, for the time being, I would stay with my consumption of raw vegetables and veggie burgers. Remember, this was not a meal plan. We were just testing the waters to see how I reacted to the ingestion of normal food, both emotionally and physically. I left Corey's office feeling hopeful.

Initially it was a total disaster. While I talked the talk, I wasn't able to walk the walk. When I woke the next morning, intending to eat a "normal" breakfast, Ana struck back with a vengeance. She said things like, *what the fuck are you doing? Do you not realize how far you have strayed off the path?* And *this is going to make you gain serious weight.* It wasn't, however, limited to the statements. When I looked in the mirror, I still saw an obese and disgusting person. My eating disorder was in control, and I felt helpless. I had no ability whatsoever to put anything in my mouth for breakfast. The positive self-talk and daily affirmations were no match for anorexia. If I ate breakfast, I would betray Ana, just like Amy betrayed me. If I ate breakfast, I would be a bad person. I would get fat. So there was no breakfast. Instead, there was the ten-mile morning, on an empty stomach, burning calories with more intensity and driven by a sense of complete failure. I now realized how powerful the illness was and that I was in for the most difficult battle of my life. My anorexic self had taken control and had let me know that I had met my match. I lost the fight that morning. So for breakfast, I ate my "safe food," that is, food that wouldn't make me gain weight. I had my typical protein bar. For the rest of the day, I had my raw vegetables, spicy sauces, and veggie burgers. After being faithful to my eating disorder, I both loved and hated Ana. I wanted to be thinner, but I also wanted to break out of the prison. Living with the contradiction drove me to the brink of another nervous breakdown. I thought at that point that I might never triumph over anorexia. The only way out was suicide and that gave me a sense of relief, because I realistically believed that I would put a gun in my mouth and blow my brains out if I came to the conclusion that there was no solution for me.

Truthfully, though, it wasn't simply that anorexia, in and of itself, had all of this power. What was really happening was that I was giving her the power to thrive and dominate my existence. I was fueling Ana because despite all of my therapy sessions, there was a part of me that didn't want to get better. I still wanted to hold on to Ana, and that allowed her to control me. Part of me still dreamed about getting back to 123.25, even though I tried to suppress and deny it. I didn't tell my psychiatrist, Elizabeth, or Corey, but it was true. I think that this was the real reason that I wasn't making any significant progress. In the early months of 2010, after all of the suffering, the contradictions, and the food restrictions, I felt, for the first time, that I really did want to get better. That desire was born out of exhaustion and frustration. I was tired of not accepting myself and loving myself unconditionally, no matter what some scale says.

I was more committed when I next saw Corey and Elizabeth. On most days, however, I was still engaging in anorexic behaviors. For example, to "cure" my body image problem, I was taking diuretics. Unfortunately, combined with the extreme exercise, this caused me to become extremely dehydrated. In fact, when I walked into Elizabeth's office for one of our sessions, I could hardly stand up, was slurring my words, and almost fainted in her office. She immediately took me to my doctor, who assessed that I was suffering from major dehydration and hooked me up to an IV. During this time, I simply fell asleep because I was so exhausted. After two hours, I felt comfortable enough to leave my doctor's office and go home, although I was still slurring my words slightly and having trouble walking. My only instruction was to drink as much water as possible (approximately 125 ounces) over the next several days to rehydrate myself. I was fine with that, but upset about the fact that both of my classes were canceled due to the fact that I was "ill." So the next day, I spent the majority of my time convincing my students that everything was fine, even though one had the audacity to say, "You look like death." This was a very scary experience for me, because, for the first time, the unhealthy effects of my eating disorder manifested themselves in such a severe way. I didn't want to die. I didn't want to permanently compromise my health. Yet, I was engaging in precisely those behaviors where that might result.

As a result of my behavior, Elizabeth and Corey came up with the idea that we should all draft a "contract" which would outline my responsibilities concerning treatment. I had to agree not to engage in excessive exercise, partake in a normal eating plan to the best of my ability, and not take any diet pills, laxatives, diuretics, or any other substances that could be harmful to my body. In addition, the contract required me to attend all scheduled sessions. Finally, if I violated the terms of this contract, then our "out-patient" treatment would stop and in-patient treatment would be recommended. Elizabeth, Corey, and I all signed the contract.

A few days later, I had another meeting with Elizabeth and, of course, the first thing I did was to repeatedly apologize for what I'd done. Elizabeth was wonderful about the whole situation, very understanding, and ready to put that behind us so that we could do the work needed for a successful recovery. During our next meeting I admitted to her that, in addition to the diuretics, I had been taking Valium as well as a "mega weight-loss" supplement. Even though I wanted to get better, I was hoping that I could lose some weight in the process. That view, however, simply reflected the control that Ana still had over my life. While that was understandable, things had to be different now. As Elizabeth pointed out, under the contract I could no longer use any "weight loss" supplements. Also, I could not starve my body by eating protein bars and raw vegetables. It was time to step up and fight the battle. There was no going back. I knew I couldn't go back, but I was petrified of going forward.

It was during our next few sessions that we began to discuss two serious events that had happened to me since we'd last talked. The theme of these events was similar: rejection. To me, when I get rejected by anything, I blame myself. That only fuels that self-hating aspect of my personality. Anyway, I have had several romantic relationships, some for long periods of time. They all failed. After the failure of my last relationship, I was content to be single and not become emotionally invested in anyone or anything. Although it was lonely and isolating at times, nothing could compare to the terrible hurt that I felt, for example, when my Erica cheated on me. However, there was another event that had recently traumatized me. I was out with friends one night at a local bar, and I noticed a girl who was the most beautiful person that I had ever seen. She was so gorgeous and had such an amazing smile that I think I then and there became a believer in "love at first sight." Her presence challenged all of my basic assumptions about love. Although I am very shy, I went up to the bar, bought her a drink, and we talked for about an hour. I was so taken aback by her beauty that it was almost difficult to talk with her, but we did in fact have a pleasant conversation. We started dating a few weeks thereafter.

We connected quickly and on a very deep level. There was nothing I would not do to make this girl happy. The sex was amazing, like something I'd never experienced. Just sitting next to her and being around her made me feel happy and complete. We spent a lot of time together, and I found myself falling more and more in love with her. We shared a lot of time together and just enjoyed living in the moment. Suddenly, though, things began to change, and to this day, I don't know why. Slowly but surely, she began to criticize me in every way possible. It started out rather innocuously, but then it slowly increased to constant criticism about my life and how I conducted myself. Now, instead of drawing boundaries and letting her know that I would no longer appreciate her incessant negative comments, I reverted back to the "people pleaser," doing anything and everything that she wanted. I would go to any lengths to make her happy and gain her approval. It didn't work. Her criticisms became more and more hurtful. She criticized the way that I talked, the way that I sat down at a dinner table, the music that I liked, the way my apartment looked, the fact that I was struggling with anorexia (which she never really understood), the foods that I ate, the movies that I liked, the fact that I was too "sweet," and many other mundane things. My response should have been to tell her to fuck off (in a nice way), but I kept letting it happen, all at my own expense. I gave her all of the power and totally failed to set any limits on her hurtful behavior. She broke up with me three months later. I had thought she was the "one." The sadness is still there. Fortunately, I've been able to let go to a certain extent, and that has allowed me to move forward.

Then, I told Elizabeth about the second problem involving, yet again, rejection. My teaching position was only on a contract-basis, so I had been seeking a tenure-track professorship for the last two years. However, I failed to receive a single offer, despite the fact that I'd received very good reviews and recommendations from my supervisors. Furthermore, my qualifications were competitive with most individuals seeking these positions. Also, I'd thought my interviews had gone extremely well. The interviewers gave me very nice compliments and feedback. However, I was never offered a position. I was both hurt and disappointed. Rejection was always a big part of my life and contributed greatly to my feeling of inadequacy and low self-esteem.

Elizabeth and I discussed these events and she explained that I should not be focusing on rejection. Rather, the way you interpret that rejection is ultimately what impacts your life. I had to ask more questions, and think a bit harder. With respect to the girl that I thought was "the one," was she really? Well, she may have been beautiful and we may have had great sex, but what was the relationship like beyond that? Was she a kind and caring person to me? No. Was she highly critical of me in many different ways? Yes. Did I constantly try to please her and was it never enough? Yes. Did I set boundaries with her? No. Did I ever stand up to the various forms of criticism that she directed at me? No. Did I give all of my power to her in the relationship? Yes. Were my moods contingent on whether she was or was not happy? Yes.

Well, then she wasn't "the one" for me at all. Instead, it was a poisonous relationship that evoked in me precisely the types of behaviors, i.e., people pleasing and not using my voice, that had led me to anorexia in the first place. I gave all of my power to another person, which enabled her to control my life in every facet. When I understood our relationship in this way, it completely changed how I reflected upon it and I viewed the break-up as a positive, rather than a negative result. I also learned that, in future romantic relationships, I would have to behave differently, engage in healthy communications, and just be my authentic self.

Now, for some reason, Elizabeth seemingly understood why I was getting rejected from all of those law schools, and she was confident that it had absolutely nothing to do with me. Elizabeth believed that being a law professor wasn't necessarily my calling in life and that there was so much more for me to do and be a part of in the future. She felt that the rejections were almost a logical result of the fact that, no matter what I did, being a law professor just wasn't "it" for me. Also, as Elizabeth pointed out, there could have been a number of reasons why I did not get these jobs, and they probably had absolutely nothing to do with me. It was just impossible to speculate. Blaming yourself only brings poisonous feelings into your life, and these are usually not accurate assessments of the situation. Indeed, the most important coping skill to learn was that the rejections were not rejections of me personally, or of my character, values, or behaviors. I performed well at every on-campus interview that I had (except one), and I should feel proud that I did the best that I could, regardless of the outcome.

That's when I learned a very important lesson: I would not take rejection personally anymore. I would look at it as a positive experience, understanding that there were reasons, maybe or maybe not having to do with me, or other factors, that led to a particular outcome. I would learn whatever lessons there were to learn and apply them to future behavior. That is the value of failure. Also, if someone doesn't want you, then it shouldn't upset you: they don't deserve all that you have to offer.

My sessions with Elizabeth were, and continue to be, invaluable. She is teaching me to assert myself again. She is teaching me to have pride in myself. She is helping me to be and to accept my authentic self. She is teaching me how to set boundaries, place limitations on the types of conduct I would accept, and to take rejection and disappointment in a way that brings me up, not down. I am learning how to have a voice again and these behaviors are not only beginning to give me a sense of self-esteem, but they have started to diminish the need for the ten-mile morning. I look forward to our weekly sessions, because they always leave me feeling empowered and emotionally stronger. When I started to think of these types of situations in a different light, coupled with positive self-talk and daily affirmation, I didn't need anorexia any more. The authentic me is enough.

I still needed to fulfill my other end of the bargain. I had to work with Corey and start eating normally again. The self-talk was critical. I had to understand that eating was normal and necessary because, particularly as an avid runner, my body needs fuel to function effectively. I had to understand that I would not get "fat" from eating one or many normal meals. To assist me, Corey would write several "self-talk" cards that I brought with me to read if I felt the urge to restrict my caloric intake. For example, some of them said as follows:

> Center yourself before food. I'm nourishing my body. My body needs these nutrients to get through the day. My body wants these vitamins and minerals ensuring that my body will be healthy in the short term and long-term.
>
> This meal is not going to make me fat. These fears are irrational. My body needs this fuel. It's ok, I'm allowed to eat. I'm not a bad person. I'm human. I'm taking the power [back].
>
> The organs need these nutrients to keep working, [and] feeding my body helps me realize my dreams and supports healing.
>
> I relax, releasing the need to control.
>
> I can trust my body and I can trust myself to feed my body. My body can trust me. I feel better and better every time I eat [and] I feel more free.

Corey also told me that, after I started to eat normal foods, my body would feel significant discomfort because, as stated above, it was not used to digesting these "new" types of foods. This could lead to bloating and "feeling" like I had gained weight, but it wasn't real weight gain, and I had to know that. She wrote a positive self-talk card expressing these feelings:

> Physical distress — it's not real weight gain — it's my body reacting to eating again. My body is very confused right now [because of the new foods being consumed] but it will pass.

So the journey began. Remember that bridge to normal eating? Well, we were back on it. This time, though, I believed I could cross the bridge. Peanut butter, jelly, eggs, Kashi cereal, oatmeal, wheat bread, seafood, sushi, fruits and vegetables, veggie burgers, and so forth. I did not necessarily mind getting back on the bridge with her support, but again, I was scared that, once my body got a taste of the foods that I had deprived myself of for years, I would outright binge on them. So we set up a plan to deal with this.

First, I would not leave any food in my house. Second, I would eat some of my favorite foods about an hour before I was supposed to see Corey and Elizabeth, which would likely deter a binge. Third, I would eat lunch at work or go out with my co-workers, which would inhibit any chance of binge eating. Corey also explained that, if I ate more food during the day, then my body would feel satisfied and I would be less likely to binge at night. In addition, the positive self-talk cards were an important preventative measure. Ultimately, my goal was to eat a satisfying breakfast, a snack before lunch, a substantial lunch, a snack before dinner, and then dinner. I was nowhere near this type of eating, but I was willing to take the first step, which is also the biggest step. I was talking the talk again and now we would see if I could walk the walk.

I also had the freedom, and the obligation, to choose those foods that I liked and to enjoy them in moderation. If I just listened to my body's hunger and fullness signals, then I would not gain weight. So, on the next day I went to my local chain restaurant and ordered scrambled eggs with a fruit salad. For lunch, I then had my peanut butter and jelly sandwich, along with blueberry yogurt. Then, I had a protein bar for a snack, and my salad with veggie burgers and a protein bar for dinner. I had done it. I had eaten normally; there was no desire to binge, and although I felt bloated and "fat" I knew, from my self-help cards, that it wasn't real weight gain. I felt so much better emotionally and physically. For the first time, I had beaten Ana, even if it was only for one day. I felt so proud of myself. Just a few months earlier, I would have wanted to kill myself for eating all that food. Now, I was ecstatic. Why? Because I started to realize that my eating disorder would have killed me. I realized it just in time. If I had gone any lower than 123 pounds, I would have been in serious trouble. I still felt like I was betraying Ana to a certain extent, but I now knew that she had betrayed me and I was doing the right thing by taking care of myself.

The next day I awoke with more confidence that I could eat normally, enjoy food, and not binge. So, I again went to the local chain restaurant and again ordered scrambled eggs with a fruit salad. I ate my breakfast, went to work, and everything was fine. I again had my protein bar for a snack and my peanut butter and jelly sandwich for lunch. This time, however, I didn't eat the yogurt because I wasn't in the mood for it. However, I did eat another protein bar as a snack and, for dinner, after going to a local bar for some drinks with a friend, I ate my salad with veggie burgers. I was happy that, for the second day in a row, I had eaten "normal" foods and neither binged nor had terrible digestion problems. I had beaten Ana for the second day in a row, and was excited to tell Corey of my progress at our meeting the next day. It was only two days of eating normal food, but it felt like two years. I was making a comeback.

So I went to sleep around 9:00 p.m., but then suddenly, I awoke around 2:00 a.m. with this ravenous desire to binge. The urge to binge was so strong that I could not resist it. I ran out of my apartment to the nearest 24-hour store and purchased five packets of blueberry and cheese pastries, two pints of ice cream, peanut butter and jelly, Reese's, and about three packets of Mrs. Field's cookies. I ran home and ate nearly all of the food. When I was finished I was in shock. *How could this happen? I ate normally today. What the fuck is wrong with me? Is this ever going to end?* I went back to sleep feeling terrible. That wasn't the worst of it. About two hours later, around 4:30 a.m., I woke up and my bed was full of vomit. I had literally vomited in my sleep and could not believe that this happened because, when I had prior binges, I never had such an episode. It was disgusting, and I was disgusted with myself. I was also scared because I could have died from asphyxiation.

The next day I had my meeting with Corey, where I was expecting to give her good news. Well, it was good and bad news. I told her that I ate normally on the first day, but on the second day, while I ate normally throughout the day, I had a horrible binge on that night. I wanted to cry. The binges hurt me so much that I contemplated suicide. However, Corey helped me so much, explaining that this was a process and that I needed to be kind and caring to myself if, and when, I binged. Corey said that positive self-talk was so important here, and she wrote another self-talk card to promote this coping mechanism:

> To get back on track (after a binge) write out the situation in a journal. Positive self-talk, kindness, support, understanding. Eat the next meal and listen to your body.

The critical thing now was to stick to our normal eating plan and not revert back to the "safe foods" that I had restricted myself to during my anorexic days. I had to put the binge behind me and move forward. So that's exactly what I did, even though it was so hard. I could feel Ana trying so hard to get me back into her cage of raw vegetables, hot sauce, and veggie burgers. I had to resist it because I deserved to be at peace with food. I deserved to be at peace with myself. I deserved happiness and a good quality of life. I deserved to be rid of the anxiety that accompanied every meal.

So the next day I got back on track. As hard as it was, I forced myself to do it. No ten-mile morning; instead, I ran only five. I had some Kashi cereal for breakfast, along with a glass of soymilk. I had my protein bar for a snack, and for lunch I had the peanut butter and jelly sandwich with Stonyhill Farms yogurt. At about 4:00 p.m., I had the same protein bars and for dinner, I had my typical salad, consisting of raw vegetables, and veggie chicken sandwiches. I utterly hated eating that day, because, after the recent binge, I viewed it as a threat to my weight, and it made me feel fat. But if I was going to get better, I had to keep trying and trying and trying. I was petrified while I was eating, because I feared that those uncontrollable urges to binge would come back. It was a feeling that if Ana decided she wanted to fuck with me and make me binge for betraying her, then there was nothing that I could do to prevent it. What I did know was that if, and when, those urges came, I would be in deep trouble. I was living in fear. I was emotionally disabled. Ultimately, after taking my Seroquel, I went to sleep and didn't wake up until 7:00 the following morning. I had succeeded again. I also took another step: I again ran five miles instead of ten. The ten-mile morning was part of the disorder, and I knew it, and I was going to put a stop to it. I was fighting Ana hard and I knew now that I had a shot at victory.

The next day I woke up in a great mood and again jogged five miles. Then I had the now-usual breakfast of scrambled eggs along with fruit. The decreased exercise and normalized food intake made me feel so much better, although I was still not getting enough calories for my activity level. I had my Clif Bar for a snack and my typical peanut butter and jelly sandwich for lunch. Then, I ate another protein bar and went to the grocery store to buy my typical dinner. After I had my typical raw veggie/meatless chicken burger dinner, I watched some TV and went to bed. Then it struck. At approximately 1:00 a.m., I awoke like a primitive animal with an uncontrollable desire to eat anything and everything in its sight. I literally felt like a crazy, unconscious creature whose only mission was to find food, and find it as fast as I could. So, it was back to the 24-hour store, the sweets, the ice cream, the Mrs. Field's cookies, the peanut butter, and whatever else I could find that looked appetizing. When I got home, I ate everything. This time, though, things went a bit differently than the last binge. As I went to bed, I immediately got a nauseous feeling and started vomiting violently all over my bedroom. I could not make it to the bathroom because I was vomiting so terribly. It was such an awful experience. If returning to normal eating was going to entail this consistent binging, then I'd gladly take back Ana.

At our next session, I told Corey the bad news. I had binged again, but this time it was worse than the last one. I had ingested an enormous amount of food in a very short period of time and vomited violently in my apartment. I thought Corey would say that this was a "natural" part of returning to normal eating, but she did no such thing. She was very concerned about the binge this time because of the violent vomiting. It was dangerous and could kill me if I was asleep. Thus, while it was in my best interests to start the return to normal eating slowly, we needed to increase my daily caloric consumption immediately to meet my activity level. I needed around 2,800-3,000 calories daily to properly fuel my body. The problem was, even though I was eating a greater variety of food, I couldn't get myself to eat even close to that many calories. I was deluding myself, to some extent, into thinking that I was eating "normally." To some degree, I was just "restricting" in a different way by eating different foods.

However, the binges and vomiting scared me. I had to make a change. If I didn't, Corey and Elizabeth wouldn't be able to help me. So I made the hardest, yet smartest, decision — to increase my caloric intake. It is now 2011, and I am eating closer to 2,000 calories per day. There are certainly days when I starve myself and excessively exercise. There are days, even weeks, when I go back to the protein bars and raw vegetables. Overall, though, I am eating more food and eating foods that I like. I go out to restaurants with friends. I've had the ability to go out and eat oysters, shrimp, and fish. I also went out for pizza with a friend of mine not long ago.

My brother, Marc, and I went for sushi, and I had the "deluxe" sushi combo. I do not count calories. I eat food even though I do not know how many calories they contain. I trust my body again to tell me when it is hungry and when it is full. Have I gained weight? I don't think so. I must admit that I don't weigh myself anymore. I don't give a scale that much power over me. I use my clothes as an indicator of what I weigh. My pants still fit me just fine. If I have gained any weight, it is probably no more than five pounds. What if I do gain more weight? Then that is my body telling me that it wants to return to its most healthy and natural weight. If it does that, then I will have a happier and better quality of life, and that is what matters most. I am still struggling, but I am in treatment and recovering. I am winning the fight. I'm now on a journey of discovering and becoming connected to my true, authentic self, and that is bringing happiness, meaning, and purpose into my life. I am developing healthy control.

While I needed Ana for such a long time, I had to let her go. I had to establish a new relationship, and that relationship was with myself and my body. I am now going to treat my body with the love, respect, and care that it deserves. I am going to love myself unconditionally, no matter what some number on the scale says. I am going to be kind to myself and my body and listen to my body when it is hungry and when it is comfortably satisfied. I am going to reconnect with my inner-self, to find the peace and calm that I deserve. I am going to have positive thoughts every day, put out positive energy, and always stay true to the real person that I am, because I love that person. I will forgive myself for mistakes that I have made and try at all times and in every situation to do the very best that I can. I will treat my body with unconditional love, and trust that my body will do the same. There is so much more to life than what you weigh.

Ironically, anorexia was the best thing that ever happened to me. Ana taught me how low into the depths of darkness one can go. I hit rock-bottom and sank into a place of horror that I never knew existed. I never would have believed that life could get so terrible. It almost killed me. Those deep, dark days humbled me and showed me that if I do not respect my life, my body, and assert my feelings and boundaries, then I could fall right back into Ana's trap. I became anorexic because I knew no other way to find a friend who would love me unconditionally. That is precisely why I created the illusion of anorexia as my best friend. Ana "loved" me and brought me control when I had none. Ana brought me love when I felt rejected. Ana brought me comfort when I was miserable. But it was all a fake world. It was a world that caused me to be so disconnected from my true self, feelings, and innermost authenticity. Ana taught me to stay true to myself. Now knowing how low and terrifying life can get and how recovery can be had under the best of circumstances, I have a humble, hopeful, and respectful approach to life, by just being me.

Chapter Nineteen

Life Lessons

Having the Strength to Dream

Recovering from anorexia has taught me to believe in possibility and to believe that I can accomplish my dreams if I stay true to myself and positive in my beliefs. My recovery has allowed me to take back power from other people in my life, and those feelings of empowerment have led to healthy ways of control and coping. For those suffering from eating disorders or other difficult problems, I want to share with you the life lessons that I learned during my journey through anorexia — how you can become a person who lives the life of your dreams, on your own terms, and in your own way.

LESSON ONE
BELIEVE

You will never recover from an eating disorder unless you genuinely believe that you can beat it. The advice sounds simple but it's not simplistic. The recovery process is emotionally and physically exhausting. It is a difficult journey that requires you to revisit your past and confront painful memories. It requires you to forgive yourself and others. It requires you to re-establish a relationship with yourself and, most importantly, food. The journey is fraught with successes and setbacks. If you believe, however, that you will recover from this illness and cross that bridge, then you will experience the true happiness and liberation that comes at the end of the road. You deserve to feel that happiness because you are unique and special.

LESSON TWO
LET YOURSELF MOURN AND SAY GOODBYE

For anyone with eating disorders, the illness not only becomes a part of our life, it becomes a part of our identity. The journey towards, and through, anorexia is filled with rejection, pain, hurt, and a sense that we have no control over our lives. All of our hopes and dreams fall apart, and we live in a reality that leaves us feeling powerless and paralyzed. For me, anorexia took away the pain. It gave me control over something, a control that no one could take away. Anorexia gave me a sense of power, importance, and accomplishment. Starvation was my salvation and the road to self-esteem. Anorexia was my best friend.

There came that moment, however, when I realized that it was all a lie. As time went by, and I started to waste away, I saw that Ana really wasn't there to save me from myself and my reality. I wasn't in control. It was controlling me. I gave Ana actually all of my power, and she nearly destroyed me physically and emotionally.

Ultimately, as difficult as this is to do, and for me it was so difficult, you have to break up and part ways with your eating disorder. You have to say goodbye. You have to come to terms with the fact that your eating disorder has betrayed you, even though it seems as if it has saved you from everything that is so wrong with this world. It feels like the death of a loved one. That's because it is. It takes time. It takes mourning. Remember, though, that this is your grieving process and you have the right to do it on your terms, on your own time, and in your own way. Some people may write a letter to their eating disorder. Some may communicate verbally. I wrote a poem, entitled "Ana," which I will share with you:

> I don't know if I chose Ana or if she chose me
> It doesn't really matter now
> Because she's taken all that matters
> .Flesh, bones, and desperation
> A reality constructed away from everything that was real
>
> Thank you for saving me, Ana
> For loving me in a way that no one else ever could or did
> You gave me just as much as you took away
> Your world allowed me to escape mine
> To live a reality where the pain is gone and meaning has manifested
>
> I love you with all of my heart
> I cannot let go even though I know I have to
> I know this world is fake and my control a delusion
> But I'm not afraid to stay

I have something now that I've never had in my heart
And for that I simply cannot go to where I've been before

But while I cannot go there my soul will not let me stay here
For now I have no choice but to say goodbye
I want to go with you and give you my life
But all I have left is flesh, bones, and certain death
As much as I love you
I need to escape

So as I mourn and say my final goodbye
Please know, Ana, that I'll love you forever and never forget
How you saved my life and made me feel like a person again
I promise to visit from time to time
And I hope you'll always be well
But most importantly I want you to know
That through anorexia you helped me discover true happiness
And avoid a life of pure hell.

Your mourning process belongs to you. Take your time and do it on your terms. But do it. You will be ok. You will learn the value of true self-acceptance, self-love, and self-respect.

LESSON THREE
SELF-ACCEPTANCE

Self-acceptance is wonderful, because it allows you to live your life truthfully and in accordance with your own passions and dreams. Self-acceptance is an ongoing process where you identify your values, beliefs, needs, desires, wants, weaknesses, strengths, limitations, and so forth. In so doing, you slowly begin to connect with you inner-self, and by that I mean, you connect to the "real" you; when you discover and embrace the "real" you, there are limitless possibilities for you to live the life of your dreams. You can, and do, create meaning for yourself.

You are a beautiful and unique person who deserves happiness. You have dreams and passions in your heart that date back to when you were young. You deserve the freedom that comes from pursuing that which makes you the person that you are. You have the right not to be judged or criticized by others. You have the right to set limitations and boundaries with those who do not treat you with respect. You have the right not to compare yourself, or be compared, to anyone else.

Self-acceptance is difficult because we live in a world filled with gossip, materialism, and falsity, where emphasis is based upon what you have, what you do, or who you are. Yet none of that matters if you are not happy. True happiness comes from self-acceptance. You have a right to love every aspect of yourself and no one, and I mean no one, has the right to say or do anything that can take that love away from you. Don't try to be someone or something that you are not, because that will only bring you further and further away from the person that you really are, and that fuels the type of self-loathing and self-hatred that blocks healthy ways of achieving self-control. When you embrace your true self, then your self-love and self-acceptance will lead to relationships where people will love you unconditionally. Self-acceptance is about truth. When you start living truthfully, you allow yourself to walk down the path of happiness, liberation, and empowerment that you deserve.

LESSON FOUR
LIVE AUTHENTICALLY

There are going to be so many people around you in your lifetime, such as friends, romantic partners, employers, and the like, who think they know "better than you" regarding what is "best" for you. Sometimes we believe that these people are right, and sometimes we act in accordance with the way others say we "should" act. Sadly, we do this even if it is at odds with our own intuition or instincts. However, no one knows how to take care of you better than you do. No one knows how to love you and decide what is best for you like you do. Your common sense, instincts, and intuition are the path you should always follow, because by doing so you are being true to yourself. You are living authentically and, as such, living freely and in harmony with the "real" you. You are entitled, and deserve, to live life according to your version of truth and meaning. Have the courage to forge your own path and take the road less travelled. When you live authentically, the word "should" can finally be excised from your vocabulary. In other words, "march to the beat of your own drum," do not conform, and never let anyone take you away from your true essence.

In addition to the "should" people, there are also going to be the "change" people. You will usually encounter these folks in romantic relationships and sometimes in friendships. These people are a sub-species of the "should" people. They consciously, and subconsciously, try to change the person that you are, to fit more within their own expectations. Sometimes the changes are subtle, and sometimes they are obvious. However, when you examine your values, beliefs, desires, and needs, you will know when someone is trying to change you. When you make that discovery, you need to know that this person does not truly like or love you for the person that you are, but instead for the person that he or she wants you to be. By seeking to change you, they are trying to disconnect you from your authentic self, so that they can place themselves in more harmony with their inner-selves. This type of relationship is the opposite of authenticity. It is falsity, selfishness, and destructive to your relationship with yourself. Nothing can be unhealthier.

You will also experience the "control" individuals, either in friendships or romantic relationships. These people feel the need to know, among other things, where you are and what you are doing at all times of the day. People like this are very dangerous because underlying their need for control is a sense of inadequacy, insecurity, and instability. These people will threaten your independence and authenticity, because of their need for you to be in compliance with all of their needs. This behavior will threaten to overpower any effort on your part to have your desires and needs met on your own terms. In a way, these people are suffering from the same underlying emotional issues as anorexics, but manifesting it in a different way.

Finally, society itself will try to challenge your ability to live authentically because it will strive to make you comply with and conform to contemporary norms and expectations. Ultimately, every person is faced with that one question of whether to conform to the common roadmap set forth by society or to forge their own way. What will you do? Will you settle and conform? Or will you follow your dreams? There is no right or wrong answer, because either choice can be right or wrong. The point is, be sure that the big decisions you make in life are based upon what you truly want and not what you think you should want. Make sure that your decisions are in accordance with your own rules, your own truth, and your own values. If you do that, then you will achieve what has been so elusive for so many people — happiness.

LESSON FIVE
DRAW BOUNDARIES AND ASSERT LIMITATIONS

I have talked about this so much because it is extremely important that people truly respect you. It is not important insofar as it has anything to do with them, but because it has *everything* to do with you. People need to feel that their family members, friends, and colleagues have true respect for them, because it enhances our sense of self-esteem and self-love. When we feel respected, we feel empowered and happy. We feel that people like us for who we are, and that only fuels our sense of worthiness. The positive energy that comes from being respected, unconditionally and without reservation, is a critical step in recovery from anorexia.

There is only one method by which to gain that respect. You have to learn to draw boundaries with people, whether they are family members, friends, colleagues, and so on. Drawing boundaries is, at its very core, about using your voice to express your feelings, emotions, agreements, disagreements, values, and beliefs. Drawing boundaries is about asserting yourself and telling others what your limitations are, namely, the things that are acceptable to you and the things that are not. Drawing boundaries means standing up for yourself as well as standing for something. In doing this, you are seeking respect. You are commanding respect, and respect is what you are going to get.

Being assertive, drawing boundaries, and placing limitations on others' actions is so important because if you do not do this, people will walk all over you, take advantage of you, and exploit you. This is the unfortunate reality of today's world, but when someone senses that you have feelings of insecurity and/or are a "people pleaser," they will use you for their own personal gain at every possible opportunity. They will sense that you do not have the ability to stand up and assert yourself. They know that they are in control and, when that happens, not only do you lose their respect, but you also lose your sense of self-respect.

LESSON SIX
ENGAGE IN CREATIVE EXPRESSION

You should always strive to live your life from the "inside-out." Within all of us, we have hopes, dreams, and aspirations about how we would like to see the world around us. For some, it might be a particular job/occupation about which they are passionate. For others, it might be about a location where they want to live, or finding that person with whom they want to spend the rest of their lives. We each have, on the inside, a reality that we wish could be expressed and realized in the outside world. Well, it can be. You are not a prisoner to your environment. You are not controlled by your environment. You have the power to change your environment from the inside-out, namely, by expressing yourself creatively, whether it is writing in a journal, writing poems, painting, relocating, searching for that dream job, or joining a particular organization.

You have the power to express and let out all of those attributes that comprise your true self, and turn them into positive action. In so doing, you change not only the perception of the environment around you, but you change the environment itself. That is the beauty of creative expression: it allows you to live in harmony with your inner-self and outside reality. By living from the inside-out, you ultimately obtain a healthy dose of self-control over your environment in a way that brings contentment, inner peace, and calm. Be creative. Express yourself. And combine it with the next lesson.

LESSON SEVEN
PURSUE YOUR PASSIONS – NEVER SETTLE

This is one of the most important gifts that you can give to yourself and to other people. It is so critical not only to be who you want to be, but also to do what you want to do. Going back to early childhood, we had dreams of what we wanted to do with our lives. Of course, as we got older, some of those dreams became quite unrealistic, i.e., not everyone can be a professional baseball player. Yet within each of us lie smaller, but just as significant, dreams and passions about how we want to live our life. Sometimes, it is difficult to pursue that which you find passionate and meaningful because so few people do, and thus the pressure to conform is very high. To make matters worse, people can view you as strange or weird for pursuing your dreams instead of following the societal roadmap. Well, sometimes you have to stand alone in fighting for what you want. At the end of the day, when you refuse to settle and you chase your dreams, the outcome never matters, because happiness is all about the journey.

When I went to law school, I wanted to become a criminal defense lawyer who fought for the rights of people who were poor and treated unfairly in our system. I believed in the notion of justice and the idea of standing before a jury and zealously arguing my client's innocence. However, I got sucked into everything that was not me: money, materialism, and status. I received good grades in law school, and all of my friends were getting prestigious jobs at big law firms across the country.

For me, that wasn't the path that I wanted to take. However, after being told all of the typical shit like "all criminal defendants are guilty," "the public defender's office doesn't pay well at all," and "most cases are resolved by plea bargains," I sold out. I settled. I didn't fight for the career that I wanted. In doing so, I formed the foundation for unhappiness. I spent the next several years practicing in areas of the law that I hated, messing around with prostitutes, abusing alcohol, snorting coke, and getting into a near-fatal accident. I did all of this because I was unhappy. I ignored my dreams and, as a result, almost destroyed myself.

I also stayed in a relationship with a married woman for too long. Even putting aside the issue of her being married, I should have ended my relationship with her the moment that she got pregnant. I was not in a loving and caring relationship. Although she was a great person, she was simply not able to care about me in the way that I needed. I deserved better. I deserved a woman who could love me unconditionally and spend more time with me, and she couldn't do that. I settled for a fraction of what I deserved. And then I got what I really didn't deserve. I felt pain every time I saw her and my self-hatred only grew, ultimately leading me to find solace in anorexia nervosa.

After these experiences, I will now never settle, and you shouldn't either. You deserve more than that. Do that which makes you happy. Fuck and forget what other people say. This is your life and you are entitled to live it your way.

LESSON EIGHT
PUT THE PAST BEHIND YOU – LET IT GO

The past can be so incredibly painful. Some of the things that have happened to us are extraordinarily traumatic and stay with us today. We have all been treated badly by others, some in ways that we will never be able to forgive or forget. The most damaging part of our past, however, is how it affects our present, and how it will impact our future. We will never be able to change the things that we have done to others or that others have done to us. Yet we can learn to understand why certain events happened and, through this understanding, move forward in a positive and liberated manner.

Sometimes, what's really troubling is that we use the present to live in the past, a place we can never return. We often look back in one of two ways. First, we may examine hurtful things that we have done to other people, and this may evoke emotions of sadness or regret. Second, we may also examine what others have done to us, and that may evoke feelings of anger and disgust. By putting yourself in either of these states, you are creating, in the present moment, a very unhealthy environment that cannot allow you to move forward with your life. So you must confront and deal with the issues in your past, forgive yourself, come to terms with what others did to you, and let it go. This is a very difficult process, but necessary for you to shed all of the negative emotions that you harbor from these experiences.

With respect to the hurt that you have caused others, it is important to forgive yourself. You are not, and never will be, a perfect person. The only thing that you can do is try to make the best decisions you can as they arise in your life. When you look back at instances where you hurt others, you need to understand that you were a different person at that time and dealing with different issues, under different circumstances. Maybe the person you are today would have never imagined doing what you did a year or two ago, but you were a different person then, who did not know what you know now. We all evolve as time goes by and gain new perspectives based upon new experiences. These experiences inform our actions and they also change us individually, so when we look back at some of our earlier actions, we may see a person that does not resemble our current self at all. That is the process of emotional and spiritual growth. You are allowed to make mistakes. Let it go so that you can now live in the present and live your life authentically.

Additionally, others have often done things to us that are so hurtful that these memories continue to haunt us to this day. So many people have been the victims of sexual, physical, and emotional abuse. Some people have been the victims of terrible crimes. Some have been betrayed by best friends. Some have had family members killed. The worst part is that these events can traumatize us for the rest of our lives. But they don't have to. You don't have to be a victim anymore. You need to confront and deal with the impact that these traumas have had on your life. You can address and express the underlying emotions that have plagued you ever since the traumatic event or events happened. You do not necessarily have to forgive what others have done to you. However, these traumas will no longer affect you. Now, you can go back to the type of "living" that you deserve: embracing yourself and living life in the moment.

LESSON NINE
DON'T STAY IN UNHEALTHY RELATIONSHIPS

Finding the "right" person to spend your life with is not an easy task. What is even more difficult, however, is finding someone you think is the "right" person, only to discover later on that he or she is not. When you make that discovery, you arrive at a critical moment: do you stay in the relationship or do you move on? Well, that certainly depends upon many factors that each of us will consider and put differing emphases on, such as how long we were with this person, how we feel about being alone and "starting over," whether we are married, have children, and so forth.

While I recognize that these factors are important, there is one situation where, despite any and all of the above factors, you should leave a relationship: when it is emotionally (not to mention, of course, physically) unhealthy for you. Unhealthy relationships come in a variety of forms and can hurt you in so many ways. For example, you may be with a person who is emotionally neglectful and/or insensitive, in that he or she is indifferent or inattentive to your emotional needs. You may be with someone that you truly love, but, ultimately, see more as a friend than a romantic partner. You may be with someone who is unfaithful to you, yet repeatedly promises that he will "change" his ways. Or you may be with someone who you have grown apart from, in that he or she no longer resembles the person that you started dating initially.

For any of these, or other, reasons, you should step back and assess whether the relationship has become unhealthy for you. Healthy relationships exist where both you and your partner truly love and respect each other. In healthy relationships, each person is attentive to the other person's needs. In these relationships, there is healthy communication. There is no feeling or belief that cannot go unexpressed. There is trust, not control, and that trust is based upon the fact that, through your personal experiences, you have both evolved together and grown closer. A healthy relationship is where your partner is both a lover and friend.

Sadly, sometimes love is not enough. The relationship still must meet your current emotional and intimate needs. An unhealthy relationship truly affects your ability to live a happy and authentic life. You deserve better than that. If you are in an unhealthy relationship, consider whether you want to stay in it — now.

LESSON TEN
BE KIND TO YOURSELF – AND OTHERS

Throughout your life, perhaps more than you'd like, you are going to make mistakes. You may forget to do something. You may perform poorly at a work-related assignment. You may say something to someone that you truly regret. Whatever it is, there are going to be times when you feel like shit about something that you have done or failed to do. The important thing is what you do after a mistake. First, admit to yourself that you made a mistake. Apologize if necessary. Then, realize that you are not perfect. Nobody is perfect. We all make mistakes. If you try to be perfect, you are guaranteed to fail. Be kind to yourself and learn the important lessons from that experience, so that you can move forward in a positive manner.

In addition, be kind to other people. Be the type of person who smiles and says hello to the person walking past you on the street. When someone makes a mistake, remember when you have made similar errors in the past, and react in an understanding manner. When someone is having a difficult time, whether it is a co-worker, colleague, friend, sibling, or parent, try to do something to help them. Don't be the type of person who has to be asked before you help someone. If someone needs something, take your kindness and positive energy and make a difference. This will bring a sense of true meaning, fulfillment, and purpose to your life. Also, by emitting positive energy, you will attract positive people, and that will form the basis for healthy, long lasting relationships.

LESSON ELEVEN
LEARN TO GIVE UP CONTROL – SOMETIMES

All of us like to be in control of our lives. A certain degree of control is healthy. That's why we have routines. We like predictability and stability. Thus, when events happen in our lives that cause uncertainty or unfamiliarity, we often become uncomfortable. We feel like we no longer have control. If instability persists for a sustained period, we may seek control in other areas so that we feel at least some semblance of normalcy. Taken to the extreme, this can result in, among other things, substance abuse and, in my case, anorexia. The need for control can be so important that it can negatively impact all aspects of our lives, especially relationships.

Importantly, however, the excessive need for control is sometimes based upon irrational fears and insecurities, and not upon any legitimate or present threat to our health or well-being. For example, I have a tremendous fear of flying and will avoid it whenever possible. If there is any chance that I can drive to a particular destination, I will. Unfortunately, sometimes I have no choice and have to fly. In the 3-4 days before my flight, I begin to get so nervous that it literally affects my ability to get through each day. The fear of flying paralyzes me. I spend time online researching plane crashes, why they happened, and whether it is likely that mine will crash. I also study the particular make and model of the plane that I will fly, including its history, when it went into service, how many times it has flown, how many "negative" incidents it has had, and whether there have been any fatalities on this type of aircraft. I could go on and on, but you get the point. On the other hand, whether I am in my new city or New York (where I was born), I will readily get into my car and drive anywhere without even thinking that I might get into an accident.

However, the facts show that you are far more likely to die in a car accident than a plane crash. This fact, however, has absolutely no impact on my fear of flying. Why? I can control my car. I am driving it and can control its speed and direction. What I don't think about is that I cannot control the potential erratic driving of others, but that is not relevant to me because I can be safe as long as I have control over the situation. Do you see how irrational my thinking is? Also, I have the awful habit of being a daily smoker, despite the fact that this habit can and does have devastating effects on my health. So why do I do it? I have control over how much I smoke, and I can try to quit anytime I want.

Thus, I am fearlessly willing to engage in acts that are far more dangerous than flying, yet my fear is placed in a situation where the likelihood of a crash is remote. So what reconciles the inconsistency? Control. My need for control is so strong because it creates in me a false sense of stability and predictability. Those attributes make me feel comfortable and safe. The problem is that my control issues are not predicated on anything rational. They are based upon irrational fears and insecurities.

It is ok to give up control — sometimes. You are flying on an aircraft designed by incredibly skilled engineers. You are being taken to your destination by highly trained pilots, who are skilled in both normal and abnormal procedures. Thousands of planes fly every day without incident, and if there are "negative" incidents, they are almost always minor and do not impact the integrity of the aircraft. In fact, flying is, statistically, the safest form of travel. This is the type of positive self-talk that I have engaged in when flying, to allow myself to give up control and place it in the hands of others. It has been a very liberating experience. It is perfectly healthy to give up control in various situations. The important aspect of giving up control is to examine a particular situation rationally, not just emotionally, and determine whether placing your trust in the hands of someone or something else is safe. When you do that, your ability to give up control becomes easier and, in the areas that you do have control, you have it for the right reasons.

LESSON TWELVE
YOU'RE NOT GOING TO GET FAT

The biggest fear I had when I began my recovery was that I was going to get fat. I had once weighed 226 pounds. I had gotten as low as 123 pounds. For me, eating normally meant eating more food, and eating more food meant gaining weight. That fear, in and of itself, almost made me initially end the recovery process. Yet I knew, deep inside, that this war was not about food. It was about unresolved emotional issues relating to my self-esteem and feelings of self-hatred.

In other words, your fear of getting "fat" is instead a fear of confronting the traumatic emotional issues and experiences that have substantially affected your life. We use food, weight, and "fat" feelings as a cover-up. It's the "way out" of, or method of coping with, painful memories. Whether through therapy, self-talk, daily affirmations, books, group therapy, or any other type of treatment, you need to confront and resolve those issues because they lie at the heart of your disorder and unhealthy need for control. When you deal with these underlying issues, you will no longer "feel" fat because fat is not a "feeling," and you won't need "fat" to protect you from these issues anymore.

You are not going to get "fat" when you return to normal eating. Your body needs a certain amount of calories each day to perform its most basic bodily functions. If you engage in any physical activity whatsoever, then your caloric needs will rise. You do not gain weight by eating more. You gain weight through substantial overeating at a consistent rate over a sustained period of time. Do you really think this is going to happen? No, it won't. Trust me, I'm going through it. I still want to be healthy and eat healthy foods. I still exercise, but more moderately. I haven't gained weight. If I do, I will trust that my body is acting in the best interests of my health.

As Corey and I continue in the transition back to normal eating, we often discuss the "fat" issue, and she has given me something helpful called "A Promise to Myself," which I will share with you.

I promise…

To always remember that I am special, important, and deserve to be loved.
To love, respect, and care for myself as well as others.
To remember that the healthy choices I make today impact the habits I create all my life.
To remind myself every day that the healthy choices I make today will eventually become habits that will affect how well and long I live.
To fully embrace my positive qualities and understand that everyone has weaknesses and struggles
To try to remember that "fat" is a substance on the body and is not an appropriate way to describe myself or another person. The word "fat" is best used as a noun rather than an adjective.
To make myself a priority in my life.
To commit myself to making the connection between healthy eating attitudes and my physical health
That each day I will try to make healthy choices that make me feel strong and good about myself.
To take the time to do what's right for my body, mind, and spirit.
To ask a trusted friend for help if I need to improve how I manage my emotional and physical health.

The only things you will gain are a new perspective on yourself, and learn to love and accept who you are.

LESSON THIRTEEN
TAKE TIME FOR YOURSELF

Anorexia is a volatile disorder. Some days you feel that you can beat it, while other times it seems so overwhelming that you feel helpless. The first thing to realize on the road to recovery is that these feelings will pass. The depressed and hopeless feelings caused by the inability to put food in your mouth will and do get better. When I was in a session with my therapist, she introduced me to the concept of meditation. I was skeptical at first, but after trying it, and now having it as a part of my daily life, I can tell you that, even after just five or ten minutes, it has quite a calming effect. While there are many forms of meditation, you can receive the benefits in the simplest of ways.

First, go into a room where there is no noise. It must be completely quiet. Then, proceed to lie or sit down, whichever is most comfortable. After that simply close your eyes and slowly feel your muscles relax as all tension is released from your body. During this time, focus on how calm and relaxed you are. Focus on your breath. Listen to your heart beating. If you would like to (you do not have to), repeat those daily affirmations over and over in your head, i.e., "I deserve to be happy," "I accept myself for the person that I am, "I love myself." Repeat these affirmations to give you a sense of inner peace and tranquility, so that when your individual meditation session ends, you will have the emotional connection that allows you to live at peace with yourself and the outside world.

LESSON FOURTEEN
EMBRACE THE QUESTIONS — AND THE JOURNEY

Sometimes it's difficult not knowing where our lives will take us. It's very easy to stay in a routine or relationship because it offers stability, familiarity, and predictability. However, we often think of wanting a better life, or starting a new life. One thing that stops us is uncertainty. Namely, we simply cannot envision the outcome of our new pursuits, or we are not sure if we would be successful in pursuing our goals. As a result, we often stay in the routines that we do have for fear of what we will lose if we venture out of our comfort zone.

This thinking only serves to defeat the purpose of living. Instead of fear, it's so important to embrace the questions and embrace the uncertainty. Embrace the journey. Embrace what it means to be alive, and embrace living your life in a way where you are striving for what you find to be meaningful. When you do that, the questions will answer themselves. And while you're doing this, remember something:

> I beg you … to have patience with everything unresolved in your heart and try to love the questions themselves as if they were locked rooms or books written in a foreign language. Don't search for the answers, which could not be given to you now, because you would not be able to live them. And the point is, to live everything. Live the questions now. Perhaps then, someday far in the future, you will gradually, without even noticing it, live your way into the answer.

Your life means something. You mean something. Take the journey.

LESSON FIFTEEN
MAKE YOUR OWN BUCKET LIST

I never did like the cliché that "life is short." It really isn't that short. We do have a significant amount of time, though we don't have as much time as we think. One thing all of us have is a list of things that we would love to do before we die. Some people do those things, while others don't. Some people say, "I wish I would have done that," or "I wish I had seen that." Don't be one of those people. The only thing that you do have is the present. You have no control over whether you will live to see the next hour, or the next day. So live each moment with your "bucket list" in mind. You know those things you've always wanted to do, those places you wanted to see, or whatever else you've dreamed of? Do it. Plan it — now. There is no reason to make excuses. You have the power to make things happen, no matter what obstacles you perceive are in your way. Once you do just one thing on your "bucket list," you'll realize that anything is possible.

LESSON SIXTEEN
READ "THE FOUR AGREEMENTS" BY DON-MIGUEL RUIZ

When I was in the initial stages of my recovery, I went through some very difficult days. I was practicing yoga on a daily basis and my instructor instinctively knew I was dealing with something difficult. After one of our sessions, he gave me a book called "The Four Agreements." He said that it gave him a new perspective on life. I read it later that day and, although it was simple in its approach, it made so much sense out of a complex world. It helped me develop a new philosophy and outlook on life. It became one of the catalysts for my recovery. It caused me to treat people differently and love myself unconditionally. It taught me how to live in this world peacefully and accept my authentic self. Please read this book. It is about adopting four "agreements" to guide your daily living, and they are:

- Don't gossip
- Don't make assumptions
- Don't take things personally
- Always do the best that you can

When you read this book, you will appreciate how these rules can lead you to live in harmony with yourself in a difficult and complex world.

LESSON SEVENTEEN
READ "THE LAST LECTURE" BY RANDY PAUSCH

Randy Pausch was a successful and well-liked professor at Carnegie Mellon University. Tragically, he was diagnosed with pancreatic cancer and given only months to live. During this time, however, Professor Pausch did something extraordinary. He gave a presentation, which was then memorialized in a book entitled "The Last Lecture." In this book, Professor Pausch discussed his childhood and the inspirational people and things that impacted his journey through life.

In addition, Professor Pausch created a list of different personal principles that governed his beliefs, values, and actions. He believed in honesty. He strived to be a fair, loving, and humble person. He also sought to be the best person he could be, and treat others with respect. Professor Pausch believed that the world was a beautiful place where you could appreciate things both big and small, and find peace in all places. The principles that are contained in his book are wonderful rules to incorporate into your daily life. They helped to make me a better person. I admire him for taking the last months of his life to truly help people. Out of tragedy came triumph, and he changed people's lives. Read his book. You can also see his lecture on the internet. It will impact you the same way it impacted me.

LESSON EIGHTEEN
FIND YOUR OWN LE BON TEMPS

Moving to and living in a new city was very difficult for me. I didn't know a single person. I felt lonely and isolated. For two years or so, I spent the nights in my apartment watching movies. During this time I occasionally ventured out to have lunch or a drink with my students, but I really didn't have any friends away from the law school. After what seemed like an eternity, I made a decision. I started driving around the city and going to different bars, coffee shops, and other places by myself. It felt a bit weird, but it was better than just sitting on my couch watching television.

One day, I found a bar not too far from my apartment. It was called Le Bon Temps Roule. I walked into the bar and loved the interior. It was what some would call a "dive bar," but to me it was an authentic bar with a great history. It was a real place with real people. For the first couple of weeks, I went there and had drinks alone, but after some time, people started talking to me. Over time, I made some of the best friends of my life. We spend some holidays together. I already have some wonderful memories. They accepted me for who I was and genuinely cared about me. It was almost like having a second family. None of this would have ever happened had I not ventured out of my comfort zone and walked into Le Bon Temps on that summer day in 2009. I can say, without hesitation, that I will be friends with these people for the rest of my life. Don't be afraid to stand on your own and try new things on your own, even if it feels foreign or uncomfortable. You might be amazed at what you find.

LESSON NINETEEN
THIS TOO SHALL PASS

For me, and for many people, it is difficult to endure uncomfortable feelings. Whether it is depression, anxiety, a broken heart, loneliness, anger, or regret, these feelings can be so painful that they cause us to sometimes engage in, or at least think of engaging in, irrational behaviors. I have had many days where the pain was so bad that it transcended the emotional, and literally turned into physical agony. I sometimes thought of suicide. You need to know, however, that these feelings will pass. You will get through these difficult times. The pain is temporary, and tomorrow is a new day with new possibilities. The cloud will lift and happiness will be waiting for you. Let yourself "feel" your uncomfortable feelings. Do not try to fight them or escape from them. Go through, not around, them, because that is the only way to heal. They will always end.

LESSON TWENTY
BE HUMBLE

Never develop an oversized ego. It is one thing to have healthy self-esteem, but it is another to think too highly of yourself. Life can be, and often is, especially difficult. For those of us who have gone through eating disorders, we know that there are sometimes forces greater than us which can threaten our physical and mental well-being. Whether it is anorexia, bulimia, drug addition, alcohol abuse, losing a job, failing a test, or anything else, always remember those times when life knocked you down. Recall, and be humbled by, the power of life to challenge you to the core, and never forget that you are never too far from what you were before. Be humble and learn from life's mistakes. Also, be humble and respectful to other people. They will love you for that, and you will love yourself.

LESSON TWENTY-ONE
DON'T BE AN ASS-KISSER – STICK TO YOUR PRINCIPLES

When I was working in corporate America, or what I find is more appropriately called the "rat race," I was so turned off by, and lost respect for, coworkers who consistently kissed the asses of their supervisors. Whether it was showering them with compliments, laughing at awful jokes that were not funny, or being the quintessential "yes" man, these people would stop at nothing to garner the good favor of those responsible for their promotions and bonuses. It was disgusting. They would do anything to advance up the corporate ladder. Not only did they kiss the asses of every supervisor around them, but they would lie and gossip about their peers in an attempt to ensure the security of their future. These people had no backbone. They were weak and pathetic. They never stood for anything, or had any principles for which they were willing to fight. No one respected them at all.

Don't be one of these people. You are special and unique. You have your own set of values and principles. In the "real" world, those values will be challenged. You may be tempted to compromise your principles in order to get a better job, a significant promotion, or a substantial bonus. You may be tempted to compromise your principles because everyone around you has done so and is reaping monetary benefits. In the end, though, even if you do receive materialistic gains, you will be living a lie. You will be fake. People will not respect you, and when you look in the mirror, or go to sleep at night, you will not respect yourself. It takes courage to stand on your own, to stick to your principles, and to remain unwavering in your values, especially when it can cost you a job, a relationship, or something else. You need to understand, however, that when you are in a healthy environment, people will respect you for precisely the values and principles that guide your life. True wealth comes from being who you are and sticking to your principles in the most difficult of circumstances. Don't be afraid to stand alone.

LESSON TWENTY-TWO
COMMON SENSE IS EVERYTHING, AND IT MATTERS MORE THAN IQ

A few years ago, after my experiences in law school and the legal profession, a thought came unexpectedly to my mind and, I must say, as unexpected as it was, I found it to be undeniably true. Basically, here it is: "the dumbest people in the world are actually those that we consider the smartest." I am referring to those specific individuals with unbelievably oversized egos, who usually work in some professional field (doctor, lawyer, architect, engineer, etc.) and think that, because of a high IQ score that they received on some standardized test, or other "achievements" that they garnered, they are better than, smarter than, and superior to everyone else. In other words, they derive their self-love from a number or letter on an exam, or some promotion that usually has more to do with politics than it has to do with merit.

Unfortunately, these people were never given a test on "life" and human relationships. Trust me, I've been around these folks for far longer than I'd like to admit. Let me tell you, as I realized when practicing law, some of them are the dumbest specimens that I have ever encountered in my life. They may be "book smart," but they really aren't smart at all. The reason is that they have no common sense whatsoever, and no emotional intelligence. These individuals have no idea how to connect and relate to others on a social, emotional, or romantic level. They don't understand how to love, listen, and respond to the inner needs of other people. They are inconsiderate and narcissistic because they believe the world revolves around their life and they need to control people to keep that little world secure. They believe that reason and objectivity govern human existence and do not understand why anyone can be unhappy if they are secure in materialistic matters. In essence, they are insensitive because they are paralyzed by a personality that does not understand the most basic concept — intelligence comes from discovering the beauty in all things big and small, in the friendship and love that you share with other people, in the bonds that we forge with others through difficult times, and in the creative experiences we enjoy as we evolve on life's journey. Life is about love and people. For those of you who are dealing with the types of people who base their egos upon everything materialistic and arbitrary, cut them out of your life. You deserve more.

LESSON TWENTY-THREE
PERFECTIONISM WILL LEAD TO FAILURE AND UNHAPPINESS

Justice Stephen Breyer of the United States Supreme Court once said, "The best is the enemy of the good." That statement could not be truer. Throughout much of my life, I was what you would call a "perfectionist." Whether it was in school, at work, in personal relationships, and so forth, I always had to be the best at everything I did. I had to be better than everyone else. Thus, for example, if I didn't receive the highest grades in my coursework, glowing compliments about my work-product, or satisfy my girlfriends in every way possible, then I thought of myself as a failure. For me, it was black and white, with no room for shades of gray. There was no such thing as second place, or "A" for effort. I would study for hours and hours, or stay at the firm day after day, just to ensure that I achieved my goal. I had no other choice — my self-esteem depended on being the best. In other words, I based my happiness on external validation, rather than any inner sense of self-respect.

Unfortunately, this approach to life made me extremely unhappy. To begin with, despite all of my academic accomplishments, as well as professional and creative achievements, I never felt that I was successful at anything in my life. People would frequently compliment me about my successes in law school, achievements as a lawyer, teaching ability, and publishing research articles. However, I never believed these compliments, because, when I examined all of these achievements, I saw nothing impressive. Instead, I saw much room for improvement. I focused on the negative aspects of my so-called "successes," whether it was the fact that I could have received a higher grade, made a better argument in court (even if we had won), garnered one or two more positive student evaluations, or been published in a more prestigious journal. In essence, being "good," or "very good" was never good enough. I needed to be perfect according to my definition of perfection. That was the only way to get the external validation which was crucial to my happiness.

That, however, was precisely the problem. Truthfully, I did accomplish many things in my life which were the products of hard work and perseverance and which were cause for me to feel happy about my effort. I was a good lawyer, I was a good writer and teacher, and I tried to inspire my students to pursue their true passions in the legal profession and elsewhere. Sadly, though, I was never able to celebrate these accomplishments. I was never able to be proud of myself for working so hard to help my students. I was never truly able to find satisfaction in whatever professional or creative pursuits I undertook, because I did not view them as perfect. Perhaps most importantly, even if I did meet my high standards and achieve a "perfect" result, I was not satisfied because there was always another challenge waiting for me which would test my abilities and threaten my self-esteem.

Perfectionism is destructive and will lead to sustained unhappiness. None of us can achieve "perfection" at everything that we do. The word "perfectionism" is not even capable of being defined. When you impose this standard on yourself, you are setting yourself up for failure and literally turning your successes into failures. It is so important to appreciate and love ourselves for the effort that we put forth in trying to succeed in school, a friendship, a marriage, and so forth. Happiness comes from accepting that it is wonderful to "do the best that you can" or "give 100%," and then be satisfied with the outcome, whether it is gratifying or disappointing.

In fact, success or failure is based not upon a given outcome, but upon the quality of the effort you expend in daily activities and relationships. If you simply do your best, then that will always be good enough because you are living your life and conducting yourself to the best of your ability. We can give nothing more than our "best" and, in doing so, you will always be able to live with the outcome. Put differently, by loving yourself based on effort rather than result, you are always a success. It is in this context that you are celebrating those "good" and "very good" outcomes that you once viewed as failures. Also, even if there are times when you did not do your best, it is ok — just get back up and keep moving forward. Life will knock you down so many times, but the key is to get back up — and keep going.

LESSON TWENTY-FOUR
WHO CARES WHAT OTHER PEOPLE THINK?

If you worry about what people will think or say about the things you do or decisions you make, then you will be paralyzed by fear, which will lead to inaction. Each of us are confronted with choices in our lives, some more significant than others. When critical choices present themselves, you will be faced with a fundamental question — will you do what makes you happy, or will you be swayed by the opinions of others? If you allow the judgments of others to influence the choices in your life, then you are allowing them to interfere with your own journey towards happiness, and no one has a right to place you in that position.

Certainly, we all have friends and loved ones who we can talk to, who will always try to help us through difficult times. It is wonderful to have these people in our lives. However, when someone seeks to impose their judgment onto you and criticizes the decisions that you make, then they are being selfish and often not trying to help you, but instead trying to impose their view of the world, values, and beliefs, onto you. Please don't let that happen. You will compromise your choices, and this will eventually lead to relationships and circumstances that are less fulfilling and meaningful. Don't worry about what others think — worry about what you think.

Epilogue

ELVIS PRESLEY

I think Jerry Schilling, one of Elvis's close friends, put it best when he said that "the problem with Elvis and Colonel Parker was not about money. It was about creativity." Ironically, although Elvis was loved and adored by so many people, I think he felt lonely, isolated, and unhappy. I truly believe that the reason for his unhappiness was similar to those that afflict most people with eating disorders. He had to live up to an image. He couldn't be his authentic self. He had to do movie after movie with the same script, concert after concert with the same songs. His creativity was stifled. Elvis felt like people didn't understand who he really was as an individual, and he didn't think that anybody particularly cared. Elvis didn't have healthy control in his life, and I think he tried to find it in all the wrong places, whether it was with other people or other things. He couldn't be his authentic self, and he used drugs to numb out from a reality that had become nearly unbearable. The drugs allowed him to escape his pain. That pain resulted from living a life that ultimately turned out to be controlled by others, who wanted to keep the image alive right up until his last concert, only six weeks prior to his death. It's such a sad story because it didn't have to happen. I love and adore Elvis, and dedicate this book to him for all of the wonderful things that he gave us, taught us, and left us with after his passing. I hope that this book provides some measure of hope and inspiration to those who are suffering from eating disorders or any type of mental illness. There is a way out — I am living proof of that.

www.ingramcontent.com/pod-product-compliance
Lightning Source LLC
LaVergne TN
LVHW090406210926
848480LV00002B/472